Christian
PEER
COUNSELING

Love in Action

Christian
PEER
COUNSELING
Love in Action

JOAN STURKIE & GORDON R. BEAR

WORD PUBLISHING
Dallas · London · Sydney · Singapore

CHRISTIAN PEER COUNSELING

Copyright 1989 by Joan Sturkie and Gordon R. Bear

Scripture quotations are from the King James Version of the Bible.

Library of Congress Cataloging-in-Publication Data

Sturkie, Joan, 1932–
    Christian peer counseling : love in action / Joan Sturkie and
Gordon R. Bear.
      p. cm.
    Bibliography: p.
    1. Peer counseling in the church. I. Bear, Gordon R., 1941–
II. Title.
    BV4409.S87   1989
    253.5—dc20
                                           89-34219
                                            CIP

ISBN 0-8499-0672-5

9801239 AGF 987654321

Printed in the United States of America

To Roy, who has been a wonderful husband for thirty-four years. Happy Anniversary. And to our eight children and son-in-law who bring us such joy: Alissa, David, Matthew, Kimberly and Kyle, Paul, Timothy, John, and Elizabeth.

Joan

This book is joyfully dedicated to my dear wife, Bonnie, and to our three other loving Bears in our life—Bryan, Lisa, and Kevin.

Gordon

Contents

Foreword

As a pastor's wife for eighteen years, I watched my husband inundated with counseling. It seemed every time we planned a family outing, some crisis came up in the church family—and he would be needed there more than with us. How desperately I felt the need of people to lift some of his counseling load. So I am thrilled that here is a book that gives a scriptural, practical, and workable answer to one of the most acute problems plaguing most pastors today—their counseling overload.

Peer counseling is such an obvious solution to this pastoral burden, with trained people providing help and support to other individuals in their everyday problems and traumas, thus freeing the pastor for the critical care problems.

While coauthor Gordon R. Bear was a young boy in our "What Happens When Women Pray Church" in Rockford, Illinois, I'm sure he observed my pastor-husband struggling to balance sermon preparation and family life with an unbelievably heavy counseling load. Now he's publishing a solution to it!

Peer counseling, of course, is just an up-to-date method of doing what Jesus taught us to do. It is what the early New Testament church practiced. And from Pentecost to now, the Christian church truly has been "bearing one another's burdens" in supporting those in grief, pain, and crisis. So peer counseling is just a way of organizing and expanding this care giving in the church today.

What a marvelous program this would be for small churches with one pastor—struggling to wear multiple hats—to the huge multi-staffed churches where pastors and professional staff find it impossible to give the needed one-on-one attention to their large congregations.

Peer counselors are just people who want to serve Jesus Christ by spending time listening to and supporting others in a nonjudgmental, confidential way. They are people of all ages, ethnic backgrounds, and social classes in the church personally caring for others of similar ages, life conditions, and backgrounds who are in need of help. They are ordinary people possessing at least some of the biblical spiritual gifts related to caring. What a fantastic use of spiritual gifts!

Training is the key to the success of this program. Some Christians instinctively know how to be effective caregivers, but others, eager to be helpful, need training. Without training, the well-intentioned personal counseling we all try to give at one time or another sometimes can do more harm than good. And there is an added bonus: this training will benefit the counselor in his or her personal life situations even if not choosing to use it extensively in a church's or organization's formal program.

I especially appreciate the authors' emphasis on a reliance on the Holy Spirit for divine wisdom, power, and love. Their suggested appropriate use of spiritual resources, such as prayer and the Bible, will ensure scripturally accurate advice rather than words from a human being which may or may not be correct, helpful, or appropriate to the specific situation.

Having experienced the tremendous power of prayer in a full-time prayer ministry for years, I was delighted to see the authors' urging a commitment to prayer by the organizers as well as regular meetings for prayer, and then soliciting prayer from other organizations. This prayer will ensure supernatural power and wisdom from God for the program.

The many illustrations of churches, organizations, prisons, etc. where peer counseling is now working should enable all of us to see the possibility of peer counseling being effective in our own churches and organizations. This book should motivate us all to initiate a peer counseling program to enable the personal disturbances of our peers to become the concern of many caring individuals—instead of just licensed professionals and overworked pastors.

What an excellent solution to the biblical mandate in Gal. 6:2 to "Bear one another's burdens!"

Evelyn Christenson
St. Paul, Minnesota

Preface

"Christian peer counselors? Who are they and what do they do?" The question was asked by a church leader who had a genuine desire to know. While some churches have excellent peer counseling programs, others are completely unaware of the benefits of this rapidly growing ministry.

This book is written for the purpose of spreading the good news that help for hurting members of local congregations is available by using their resources (people) who are trained, capable, willing, and able to serve Christ through a peer counseling program. Our testimony is that this is a vital, worthwhile ministry. We are encouraged by the overwhelming, positive response of people we come in contact with who share our position. The research from major universities and seminaries also verifies that peer counseling is effective in helping persons with life's problems.

At the Christian Booksellers' Convention in Anaheim in July 1987, the coauthors of this book met for the first time. Each of us had worked in the peer counseling field (Gordon as a consultant to churches and Joan as a peer counseling teacher and consultant to schools and churches), and we were interested in combining the knowledge and experience we had to create a book for peer counselors, counselees, and leaders in churches and parachurch organizations. Both authors are pleased, as well, to offer a contribution to the secular mental health field and the non-Christians in the peer counseling movement. Lastly, it is our hope that the book will find its place in the libraries of teaching centers as a unique endowment to the literature of peer counseling.

This book is divided into four sections. It may be used in its totality, or each of the four parts may be used separately. The first section contains the legacy of the Christian church and the history of the peer counseling movement, while the second section covers the vital components of establishing and maintaining a program and the overview of a training sequence. Through years of experience, research, and interviews, we have gathered and presented information from actual peer counseling ministry models, and in the third section we have told anonymous, yet true, stories, with permission from counselors and counselees of Christian church programs. In the fourth section, hoping to help churches and parachurch organizations, we have included sample forms, program ideas, and our extensive bibliography.

Selected parts of chapters three and four have been presented by the authors at the first International Congress on Christian Counseling held in Atlanta, Georgia, in November 1988.

We want to thank all the peer counselors, counselees, and leaders of churches and parachurch organizations who have allowed us to use their materials and their life stories. It is through their cooperation that this book is possible.

And certainly we want to thank our families who have been a constant source of encouragement, support, and love. You are the best!

Joan Sturkie
South Pasadena, California

Gordon R. Bear
San Diego, California

Part 1

Introduction

1

The Legacy of the Christian Church

"Goodbye, Pastor Brooks. Thank you again for listening. I really needed to talk to someone today." The strain of the past few weeks could be heard in the young woman's voice and seen in the emptiness of her eyes. Grief has a look all its own, and losing a husband suddenly in a car accident had left an indelible mark on Mary's face. Glancing out the window as she pulled her coat around her slender shoulders, Mary remarked in an apologetic voice, "I didn't realize it had gotten so late. The sun is already down. I hope I haven't kept you from your dinner."

As he opened his office door, Pastor Brooks reassured Mary that she had not kept him from his evening meal, but before she had time to cross the room to the outer office door, it swung open, and a middle-aged man in khaki work clothes hurried through. He hardly noticed Mary leaving as he rushed past and went directly, unannounced, into the pastor's study.

"I can't go home tonight and face Helen," he exclaimed before Pastor Brooks could invite him to sit down. "She doesn't deserve this. Isn't having leukemia bad enough without having a husband who has just been laid off?" Without waiting for the pastor to answer, he continued, "We barely have enough money to meet our bills, especially with the high cost of the new medication Helen is taking. How can I tell her that I don't have a job to go to tomorrow?"

An hour later, Pastor Brooks walked this latest visitor to his car. Putting his arm around his parishioner's shoulder, he offered one last word of encouragement before turning to walk back to the church. There was no time to return to his office now. The deacons' meeting would start in five minutes, and he made a practice of always trying to be on time for all meetings.

The events of the day flashed through his mind as he made his way across the cold asphalt of the parking lot. Had it been this morning that Mrs. Cunningham had intercepted him at his car as he parked in his designated place? So much had happened since 8 A.M. It seemed as if some of it must have happened yesterday. But it hadn't. Mrs. Cunningham had started explaining to him before he got out of his car that she had waited up all night for her sixteen year old to return home. There had been an argument between mother and daughter, and the teenager had stomped out in anger, telling her mother that she was running away. At that time Mrs. Cunningham had not believed her, but she did now—and she was frantic! Raising a teenager alone was something she did not feel prepared to deal with, but she had no choice. Two years previously her husband had announced that he had found someone else and wanted a divorce. Now she was all alone, desperately in need of someone to talk to, someone to care.

Continuing to recall the day's schedule, Pastor Brooks remembered that his eleven o'clock conference had been scheduled in advance. But having an appointment did not make Mrs. Evans's problem any less serious. Mrs. Evans had to make a very difficult decision concerning her aged mother. Should she put her in a nursing home as her husband was insisting that she do? In three weeks Mr. Evans would retire, and he wanted his wife to be free to take the long-awaited trips they had dreamed of and saved for most of their married life. Or should she comply with her mother's wishes and stay at home so her mother could remain with her? What if something happened to her mother while she was away on a trip? Would she ever be able to forgive herself? But what about her husband? Didn't she have a responsibility to him too? She felt she must talk this out with someone, and it couldn't be her husband or her mother.

Having reached the church building, Pastor Brooks stopped and bowed his head before opening the door to go to his next meeting. The frustrations of the day were apparent as he said in an audible voice, "Oh, God, help me to meet the needs of these people. You know I'm spending more and more time away from my own wife and teenagers, but the problems of my parishioners seem to be multiplying faster than I can keep up with them. If only there were two of me so I could duplicate my efforts!"

This cry is being heard across the nation today, and it is voiced not only by pastors, but by leaders in Christian organizations as well. Is there a solution? Can the caring and supportive efforts of pastors and Christian workers be duplicated? Tripled? Quadrupled? The answer is yes—if caring people are trained to be peer counselors.

Never before in history has the time been better for Christians to reach out and uphold their fellowman in care and love. True, the needs are many and the challenges are great—but so are the opportunities.

Newspapers, radios, and televisions report violence in the home, crime in the streets, and even shootings on elementary school playgrounds. Church members find themselves faced with problems in their own lives relating to marital discord and divorce, alcohol and drug abuse, sexual discrimination, anorexia, teenage pregnancy, illness, and death. Where are they to turn to find an outstretched hand, a head bowed in prayer for them, and a listening ear? To pastors and mental health professionals, of course. But let's take a look at what is happening to these overworked people.

As concerned and caring as pastors and their staffs are, they have come to the full realization that the task of meeting the needs of their parishioners is too overwhelming for them to handle alone. Some churches have initiated peer counseling programs because the pastor was close to a physical or emotional breakdown after years of unrelenting pressure and exhaustion. One person can try only so long to fill the super-human role of answering the numerous needs of the people. These pastors are the first to report that blessings beyond all expectations have come to them when peer counselors are available to help. Their pastoral counseling load has become lighter, while at the same time more parishioners are receiving help. With a smile, they are also admitting that peer counselors are doing a better job, in many instances, than they were able to do. Not only do the peer counselors represent more hours of available counseling time, but they also provide a wider variety of life experiences to which the counselee can relate.

Professional mental health workers are also finding that the demand for their services is more than they can meet. Clients with daily living problems are taking the time professionals sometimes need for people with severe emotional illnesses.

Since the pastors and their assistants, parachurch organizations and their staffs, and mental health professionals all admit they are overworked and can not carry the burden alone, someone else must be found to listen and care. That someone else is the lay person who can relate and help. And often that person can relate even better than anyone else because he or she has previously experienced a similar problem. A widow knows the pain of another widow; a recovering alcoholic can relate to the temptations of another alcoholic; one parent is aware of the frustrations of another parent. There are many advantages of going to a peer who understands. A rapport is quickly established, and a trust is built.

And where does one find these caring people who will become peer counselors? They are found in Sunday school classes, adult and youth groups, Sunday morning and evening services, Wednesday night prayer meetings—in all the pews of the Christian churches. These people are plumbers, secretaries, schoolteachers, housewives, dentists, insurance salesmen, chefs, mechanics, doctors, firemen, butchers, hairdressers, lawyers, businessmen and women, nurses, social workers, janitors, police officers—the list is endless. Caring people are found in all walks of life. They may be young or old (or somewhere in between), rich or poor, extroverted or introverted, beautiful or homely. These are people who are no different from anyone else. The only thing that sets them apart is the training they receive which enables them to know how to respond more appropriately to peers in need. After they are trained, accepted, and commissioned, they serve as peer counselors. And what makes this exciting is that **you**, too, can be one of these caring people. **You** can be the one who can make a difference in someone's life. **You** can become a peer counselor—a person trained to listen and help his or her peers with everyday problems of life.

You may be one of the many Christians who asked during times of trouble, "Why, Lord? Why me?" The answer may not have come then, and it may never come. But one thing is certain: with God's help you can come out of those bad experiences with more strength and understanding—and greater empathy for others. These positive tools can be used in your work as a peer counselor to relate to people who are having a similar experience. As one woman stated, "I could not talk to anyone. No one else could possibly understand my pain. Then Peggy knocked at my door, and I knew someone did understand. I would be able to talk to Peggy. She, too, had lost a teenage daughter."

But you may be asking, "What about the people like me who have not had major problems in their lives? Can we, also, become peer counselors?" Of course. People can be good listeners and helpful servants without having experienced all the traumas of life. God can use you as a peer counselor, as He uses others who have basically trouble-free lives.

The opportunity to be a part of this peer counseling movement is available to all people and to all churches. Peer counseling is for everyone. One of the authors of this book first witnessed the amazing success and power of this program on a high school campus. With the knowledge that teenagers were certainly capable and effective in helping each other, she then became interested in seeing if it worked as well with adults, especially in the churches. What she found convinced her that (1) yes, it certainly is as effective with adults as it is with teens, and (2) if peer counseling is used **any** place, it should be in the churches. The Christian church and parachurch organizations are the natural places for people to show care and concern, to help the members with their day to day problems.

History has shown that the church has always been the initial leader in building hospitals, establishing schools, and providing for homeless children. What an opportunity for the church to step out now, as it has in the past, and to take its rightful place in the forefront of this movement, providing leadership in meeting the needs of not only its own memberships but of other people in the community as well.

Peer counseling is a new exciting statement of an old idea. It speaks to the Christian heart. Faith is demonstrated in works. Love is put into action. Needs are met. Christ is glorified. This is an opportunity for Christian people to serve and for the world to see the love of Christ shining through each peer counselor. This is an opportunity for you.

But, before you become involved in this movement, you will want comprehensive answers to the following questions: What is peer counseling? Is it just a new fad that is going around? Is it Scriptural? Should it be used in the churches and in Christian organizations? What would Christ have us do?

All these questions and more will be answered in the

remaining pages of this book. But let us start at the beginning with the caring ministry of Christ and the legacy of the church.

THE CHRISTIAN LEGACY

The life and teachings of Jesus Christ present to the world a supreme model of care giving and service to others. In one of his sermons, the Apostle Peter aptly described Jesus Christ as "one who went about doing good" (Acts 10:38).

On the memorable night that Jesus was to be betrayed, he modeled for his twelve disciples the ministry of a servant by washing their feet. He admonished them to follow his example by serving each other as he had served them (John 13:15–17).

Jesus gave his disciples a commandment "to love one another, as I have loved you," and He told them that by their love one for another, the people of the world would know they are His disciples (John 13:34–35).

This legacy of care giving and service to others was demonstrated, in fact, by the disciples and early church by their loving fellowship and communal life of sharing resources with each other according to their respective need (Acts 2:41–47). The early church was a support group of caring relationships that provided the human contact for the spiritual outreach of God in evangelism, discipleship, and church growth.

The legacy of caring is truly represented in the ministry and writings of the Apostle Paul, who became one of the church's first missionaries to the world and probably the greatest church builder in the history of Christianity. Paul continued the central teaching of Jesus Christ with his message "to love one another" (Rom. 13:8; 1 Thess. 4:9), and he promoted a quality of interpersonal living in the church so that "the members should have the same care one for another" (1 Cor. 12:25). Paul's ministry of care giving is summarized in the following teachings: "Bear one another's burdens and thereby fulfill the law of Christ. . . . We that are strong ought to bear the infirmities of the weak. . . . As we have opportunity, let us do

9

good unto all men, especially to them who are of the household of faith" (Gal. 6:2; Rom. 15:1; and Gal. 6:10).

The history of the Christian church from the day of Pentecost to contemporary times has been a legacy of care giving and service to others. This history of helping and healing the poor, broken hearted, infirm, and oppressed is documented in books such as Clebsch and Jaekle's *Pastoral Care in Historical Perspective* and Oden's *Crisis Ministries*. There is not an extensive history concerning the functions of the church in terms of membership care, but it is clear that the legacy of care giving continued down through the centuries to our present time.

In the contemporary church the legacy of care giving has continued in a variety of people-helping services and programs, such as food pantries, clothes closets, hospital visitation, parenting classes, marriage enrichment weekends, and day care programs. Basic to most churches is pastoral care and counseling for the membership and other people in the community at large. Along with pastoral counseling there is an increasing acceptance and use of professionals such as psychologists, social workers, and nurses. Furthermore, there has been a development of care giving among lay people providing the church with the ministries of lay shepherding, support or care groups, and lay or peer counseling.

Peer counseling then is just another extension in this legacy of caring. More specifically, in the United States it has been a part of church and Christian communities since the 1970s. Before that time, we have to look outside the church for the literature, the approach, and the methodology in the peer counseling movement that has been developed by the professions and human resource agencies. The churches have been flexible and adaptive enough to take to themselves those methodologies and approaches, learn from them, and apply them in their ministries.

Given the legacy of care giving and servant ministry within the church, it is the intent of this book to provide a systematic and thorough understanding of peer counseling, so that it can be more comprehensively understood and more efficiently used by the churches in caring for their members and other people in the community who would look for a message of hope and a means of help. The present success of peer counseling in some churches and Christian organizations suggests that it will spread to others.

REALIZING THE LEGACY AND TODAY'S CHRISTIAN

The questions that come to most church members are, "Does this legacy include me? And if so, how can I, when I feel so insignificant, be used by God to be a link in this important chain?" The fact is the legacy has been brought down through the years by people who consider themselves ordinary Christians, usually quiet men and women who go about their lives without the fanfare of trumpets or expectations of recognition. But their degree of caring and service elevates them from the rank of the average Christian to the pedestal of honored servant, with their status often known only by God. They walk with a confidence and an inner glow that expresses itself through the tranquility seen on their faces.

Some Christians seem to know instinctively how to reach out, listen, and be supportive, but this is not true of all. Others want to serve but are able to do so only after much trial and error. This method proves frustrating and discouraging, not only to themselves, but to the recipients of their efforts as well. Still others find expressing their caring difficult and think of themselves as being so inadequate that they give up before they begin. In this latter group, there are many potential caregivers who are lost to service simply because they have not had training to equip them to know how to serve.

An example of this problem is seen frequently when a friend or acquaintance has experienced the death of a loved one. At this time, when expressions of caring are most needed, friends find themselves unprepared to reach out, comfort, or offer words of condolence.

11

Sarah fit into this category. She and Betsy had been friends since childhood. With each marrying a local boy and remaining to live in the community, it was easy to continue the friendship. Meeting about once a month to drink coffee at one of their kitchen tables, they sometimes reminisced about their high school days while their toddlers played at their feet. They seemed to be able to talk openly about anything that concerned them, from raising children to stretching the family budget. When Betsy's younger sister drowned in a freak boating accident, all of a sudden Sarah found herself mute. After she received the phone call from her mother, she wanted to call Betsy immediately—but she hesitated. After all, Betsy was a member of a large family, and they would all be getting together. Sarah rationalized that Betsy would have plenty of support.

When the day of the funeral arrived, Sarah wanted desperately to go up to Betsy and give her a hug, but she refrained. She didn't know what to say, and she certainly didn't want to make matters worse by saying the wrong thing. It would be safer to remain at a distance—so she told herself. Besides, a lot of people were approaching Betsy, and she wouldn't notice that Sarah wasn't there. How easy it was to continue to rationalize, once one started.

In the weeks that followed the funeral, Sarah found it to be more and more difficult to pick up the phone and invite Betsy over for their usual cup of coffee, so she postponed the invitation, week after week, feeling more guilty each time.

Betsy missed having talks with Sarah, but she didn't call her. She just sat at home with her thoughts: something must be wrong for her friend to act so strangely. She had looked for Sarah at the funeral but did not see her. If only she had come up and just given her a hug. Words weren't necessary. Just a hug would have done. She must have misjudged their friendship—Sarah must not have been the friend that Betsy thought her to be. Even so she still really missed her, especially now. How she needed one of their talks!

Sarah opened her Bible to Galatians and started to read the sixth chapter. She had gotten only to the second verse when the words seemed to jump from the page, "Bear ye one another's burdens, and so fulfil the law of Christ." Burying her head in her Bible, she confessed in a broken voice, "I want to, God, but I don't know how—I truly don't know how."

Sarah's words are not unique. They are voiced over and over each day by Christians across the country. Whether they are voiced audibly or inaudibly, the desire remains the same.

Training is necessary, and a skill is needed. Having to develop these skills should not seem unnatural. One acquires skills in other areas. Why not develop them in communication, something fundamental to all people? Once these skills are acquired, they are available whenever they are needed.

When two people are trained, one may choose to use the skills very frequently, while the other person may hold them in reserve, to be used only when needed. Both of these people, however, play important roles in their Christian service.

There is also a side benefit to being trained as a peer counselor besides knowing how to help someone else: one begins to understand himself or herself better. Sarah needed to know not only *how* to reach out to Betsy but also *why* she wanted to keep her distance. Knowing that what she felt was often experienced by others would have erased some of her guilt feelings.

Most people do not know that the theory of "contamination by association" sometimes is used unconsciously when a tragedy occurs. By not associating with Betsy, Sarah would not be "contaminated" and thus made vulnerable to the fact that a tragedy could occur in her own life. If she kept her distance, she would not have to come face to face with the reality of death. If she acknowledged that Betsy's sister could die so suddenly, then she must acknowledge that she could lose her own sister just as suddenly. Keeping her distance made it easier for her to remain in a denial of reality.

13

If learning about oneself, then, is a side benefit of the peer counseling training, why not let anyone who wants to be trained do so? While it is true the church or Christian organization may need only a certain number of peer counselors at any one time, the fact remains that the training is beneficial to everyone. It would be well for the participants to know that taking the course does not guarantee everyone will be chosen automatically to be used as peer counselors in the counseling ministry of the church or organization. However, improving communication skills will be beneficial in many different areas of their lives: at work, home, or school. Some people may discover, after taking the course, that counseling others is not what they had anticipated it to be and feel led to spend their time in other areas of Christian service. Needless to say, their skills will be used automatically in their daily lives at some time or another, whether they actually intend to do formal counseling or not.

Peer counseling does have something for everyone. While the legacy of the church in caring has been passed down from generation to generation, the opportunity for active participation in this chain is greater now than it has ever been. This is true because people who have believed themselves to be inadequate in the "know how" of care giving can now be trained and given preparation in the development of the necessary skills.

2

The Peer Counseling Movement

In addition to this legacy of Christian caring, there has been in the United States a movement that now can be called the peer counseling movement. Beginning with the post World War II years of the behavioral science disciplines of psychology, psychiatry, psychiatric nursing, and psychiatric social work, there developed a professional methodology and an approach for helping people who had troubles. From these disciplines a range of services and modalities became accepted and later constituted what are now known as mental health services, for example, counseling, group therapy, and half-way houses.

A second impetus of the peer counseling movement resulted from a revolution in the mental health and social services that became obvious in the United States in the 1960s when the human resource organizations began promoting the use and effectiveness of lay people, paraprofessionals, and indigenous workers as caregivers. These organizations, for example, trained an indigenous gang member to work within the gang structure to get the members to become less destructive by working with each other. Gang members were used to try to promote a sense of care and peer help. Indigenous caring also came into mental health programs in hospitals and other facilities when they began to use patients in a buddy system to help each other. In such programs, a recovering alcoholic or a sober drug user on recovery would help another drug abuser with a similar problem.

The human services revolution also discovered that efficient care giving and substantial help does occur in the natural networks associated with individual lifestyles. A natural network would be a family, a kinship system, a friendship group, a school, or a religious organization. Even more informal associations, such as those between bartenders, hair dressers, and their patrons, were duly recognized for the support they gave to people in trouble.

A major contribution of the mental health revolution was that care giving for personal disturbances became the concern of all individuals and not just the licensed specialists or professionals. In the 1960s there were training programs and certifications given to people who were not highly trained but somewhat skilled in helping in a variety of ways. These people in this new care giving discipline were known as peer counselors.

The peer counseling movement was established in the United States during the 1960s and 1970s from the work of Robert R. Carkhuff, Gerald Egan, and A. E. Ivey. These counseling practitioners provided the philosophy, theory, value base, and skills for training nonprofessionals to be caregivers as peer counselors.

Peer counseling is now an organized and institutional type of service existing across the United States in a variety of social organizations such as elementary and secondary education, universities, law enforcement agencies, and nonprofit community resources. Peer counselors are people of all ages, ethnic backgrounds, and social classes. The common denominator for this diverse group is their personal caring for others in need of help.

Because of the awareness of increasing problems with teenagers such as suicide, drugs, pregnancy, truancy, and school dropouts, educational institutions developed caregiving services. After trying many different approaches, educators concluded that peers listen to peers, and that the most effective resource they had were the teenagers themselves. Dr. Stuart Gothold, Los Angeles County Superintendent of Schools, was one of the first influential educators to recognize this resource. In an article for a parent-teacher newsletter he said, "I think there is a message offered by peer counseling. The message is that as the world becomes increasingly complicated—which it will—adults may become less and less equipped to deal with the complex feelings of young people as they grow up. Peer counseling suggests that in some cases it may be a good idea for adults to admit they are overwhelmed, not feel guilty about it, and find other ways of helping. In this case—and in many others—that help could come in the form of helping kids help other kids. After all they do speak the same language."

Educators were instrumental in getting peer counseling into their curriculum, but help in making the programs successful was given not only by educators but also by mental health personnel. Again there is an integration of two different groups coming together for a common goal. Dr. Michael Durfee, Coordinator of Child Abuse Prevention Program, Los Angeles County Department of Health Services, states, "The realities of life and the limitation of school resources call for the expansion of peer counseling to all campuses. Students are a resource. They can be a damaging influence on each other's lives or become a powerful force for thoughtful action. Peer counseling creates a platform for the latter. It provides a foundation for constructive behavior both in school and later throughout their lives."

While peer counseling was used in schools to some extent in the 1960s and 1970s, it has been the 1980s that has seen it really flourish. An example of this would be the number attending the California Peer Counseling Association Conference. This association was formed in 1984, and six hundred attended the first conference held in the spring of 1985; the second conference in 1986 had eleven hundred attending, and the third in 1987 had more than twenty-one hundred. The Los Angeles Convention Center was a beehive of activity as students, teachers, counselors, and administrators came together to share information and gain knowledge to take back to their own school districts. This excitement was repeated as the fourth conference was held in San Francisco, with more than three thousand in attendance.

Peer counseling state associations are now in existence across the nation, with each having their own conferences to help the movement grow in their state. In 1985, the number of peer counseling programs in elementary and secondary schools was estimated at more than ten thousand. By 1988 the estimate was that the number had doubled.

In April 1986, the National Peer Helpers Association was founded, and in June 1987, the first national conference was held in St. Louis, Missouri. Thirty-three states were represented when people came from their elementary and secondary schools, universities, social agencies, and churches. With peer counseling programs growing rapidly in the educational world and the excitement of the conference mounting, the pastors, ministers of youth, and students in attendance carried a new vision of service back to their churches.

The Spring 1988 issue of the California Peer Counseling Association newsletter carried an article by Anne Herrick. In it she stated, "Overwhelmed! That is exactly how I felt after a month as Youth Minister at Our Lady of Guadalupe Parish in La Habra, California. Having worked with youth for ten years, I was already aware of the issues youth deal with. However, I had never worked in a parish with 4,500 families. I wondered how I alone could possibly meet the needs of approximately 1,000 youth. Frustrated at my circumstance, I began to seek out solutions for my situation. This is the history of the birth of the O.L.G. Peer Counseling Program." She goes on to say later in the article, "After five months of offering our program, it is really beginning to take off. The future of the program looks great and more and more youth are eager to become peer counselors. I am proud and confident of our young counselors. They are well trained and competent and we have really offered a service for our community."

Another distinct example of the peer counseling movement came through the law enforcement agencies. As early as 1955, the Chicago Police Department developed a service for employees who were troubled with alcoholism. Also, the Boston Police Department began an informal alcoholism counseling group in the early 1950s. It was modeled after Alcoholics Anonymous and utilized a system of mutual support between admitted alcoholics. Officers felt they could trust peers over professionals, and the agency promoted the fact that one employee could help another in this area.

Thereafter, police departments around the country developed their own programs: the New York Police Department in 1966, the Los Angeles Police Department in 1968, and the Los Angeles Sheriff's Department in 1983. These programs are now developed more comprehensively to include budgets, manuals, training, and staff. Peer counselors are trained to meet various needs of employees in areas such as drug and alcohol abuse, divorce, death and dying, family problems and relationships, stress, and retirement.

The Los Angeles County Sheriff's Department reported that from March 1, 1985 through December 31, 1987, more than 2,025 face-to-face counseling sessions were conducted with departmental personnel, their family members and/or significant others. This number does not include the 971 times assistance was rendered over the telephone. During this same time period, the most common concerns brought to the peer counselors' attention involved marital problems. The next most common, in descending order of times seen, were bereavement, alcohol dependency, career concerns, disciplinary issues, suicide, religious/spiritual guidance, medical problems, conflicts with coworkers, financial concerns, supervisor/subordinate issues, relationships with step-children, and off-duty disability.

Social agencies are another prime user of peer counselors. The Dallas Lighthouse for the Blind is one example. Some unique hurdles were overcome to make this a successful program. While transportation is normally not a problem in most peer counseling programs, with visually impaired peer counselors this was not the case. To attend meetings or visit a counselee, they would need to be driven by a friend or take a taxi. When the latter form was used, the money for the fare was always provided by the peer counselor. The benefits outweigh the problems though, as visually impaired senior citizens report they have a new interest in living because they once again feel needed and useful.

Other social agencies using peer counselors include the Austin Child Guidance Center in Texas, Teen Line in Los Angeles, Child and Family Services in Honolulu, the Metro Center YMCA in Seattle, and the Senior Citizens Center in Santa Monica. As can be seen, the age groups of the peer counselors extend from teenagers to senior citizens.

Businesses soon recognized the effectiveness of having trained peer counselors. Companies documented the fact of financial gain as a result of peer counseling from a reduction in worker compensation claims, loss of employees and associated replacement cost, and sick leave time. They found the employees had a boost in morale, while the company had a rise in the overall quality of the work climate. One of the major business enterprises using peer counselors is the Security Pacific Bank in Los Angeles and its branches throughout California. In the first 4 months of their program, bank volunteer peer counselors spent a total of 150 hours helping 60 employees with problems ranging from how to handle well-meaning coworkers who wish to express sympathy to the employee with cancer to how best to approach teenage children when the parent suspects drug abuse.

Educational institutions, social agencies, and businesses have discovered they all have a common objective: to help their people who have personal problems. They are reaching their goal by training peer counselors to be available when a need arises.

PEER COUNSELING COMES TO THE CHRISTIAN COMMUNITY

The church and parachurch organizations began to look to the peer counseling movement during the 1970s. The theological and institutional antecedents to the readiness for peer counseling came from the church renewal movement, which emphasized spiritual gifts, body life, and social activism. It began in its earlier form with the pastors and rabbis receiving psychological training and going to their churches and synagogues offering a level of mental health services to their parishioners.

Training by clergy for their deacons, deaconesses, and elders to help fellow parishioners has been the result of the pastoral care movement. This became more specifically expressed when Christians went into the mental health professions, such as psychology and social work, and began to take an interest in helping, by using their professional expertise, the troubled people in the church. They eventually developed counseling centers at churches and training programs for care giving among members.

The practical demand for peer counseling came directly from rank and file church members who personally struggled with such painful realities as child abuse, teenage alienation, depressed wives, overburdened husbands and mid-life crises, lonely singles, and the unwanted elderly. They were people who experienced the unfortunate truth of the Scriptural statement, "woe to him who is alone when he falls and has not another to lift him up" (Eccles. 4:10).

21

Leadership in the Christian peer counseling movement came from gifted evangelicals in pastoral and professional counseling disciplines (psychology, social work, and psychiatry). The centers of influence included people like Jay E. Adams, Gary R. Collins, H. Norman Wright, Stanley E. Lindquist, Lawrence J. Crabb, Jr., John W. Drakeford, Paul M. Miller, Paul Morris, Paul R. Welter, and Richard P. Walters. These leaders helped the church and parachurch organizations discover a new biblical mandate for bearing one another's burdens (Gal. 6:2).

Christian counseling professionals across the country pioneered the development of peer counseling training programs in response to the needs of the church and its members. In 1973, Dr. Stanley E. Lindquist, clinical psychologist and founder of the Link-Care Foundation in Fresno, California, began a peer counseling training program at the Link-Care campus. The program had, for many years, a very successful church training center at the Evangelical Free Church in Fresno (the Ashlan Institute). Dr. Lindquist published a skills manual for peer counseling training in 1976 for use by church laity.

An excellent contemporary congregational model is the Neighbors Who Care Lay Counseling Ministry of the Neighborhood Church (Assemblies of God) in Bellevue, Washington. This ministry began in 1975 by Jack V. Rozell and Dr. Ray Vath, a psychiatrist, to assist in the pastoral care ministry of the church. The New Directions Counseling Center in Concord, California, is an outstanding parachurch peer counseling organization. Founded in 1974 by clinical psychologist Dr. Robert C. Richard, New Directions continues to provide Christian paraprofessional counseling to low income people.

National training programs now exist in various parts of the country offering formal classes or seminars to lay people for certification in Christian peer counseling. The most extensive and widely acclaimed training program for local churches is the Stephen Ministries of St. Louis, Missouri. Dr. Kenneth

Haugk, a minister and clinical psychologist, began this training program in 1974, while serving as associate pastor at St. Stephen Evangelical Lutheran Church in St. Louis.

Dr. Barbara B. Varenhorst has also made contributions to Christian peer counseling. A leader in the peer counseling movement since the early 1970s, she first became prominent as the director of the Peer Counseling Program for the Palo Alto School System in California. Dr. Varenhorst began to consult in 1982 with the Board for Youth Services of the Lutheran Church, Missouri Synod. This consultation lead to the introduction of youth peer counseling to synod churches. In 1988, Dr. Varenhorst, with Lee Sparks, wrote a valuable book, *Training Teenagers for Peer Ministry*. This book is a step-by-step training manual for adolescents in how to care for other teens.

The first International Congress on Christian Counseling held in Atlanta, Georgia, during November 1988 was a significant event in the history of the peer counseling movement within the church. Lay counseling was one of nineteen major program tracks of the Congress, with eleven workshops. Some of the important papers from this congress will soon be published as curriculum for training lay counselors and as a biblical approach to equipping Christians for a helping ministry.

While the name of peer counseling may sound new, the concept has been with us since the time of Jesus' earthly ministry. God has provided for the Christian community a body of literature and a proven approach for caring that matches the biblical care-giving principles set forth by Jesus and the writing of the Apostles. Undoubtedly, peer counseling represents one of the best approaches to caring that can be naturally and practically used by the Christian community to enlarge its own legacy of caring.

Part 2

Establishing a Good Peer Counseling Program

3

Components of a Quality Peer Counseling Program

This chapter will present eight general components that constitute a quality peer counseling program. A ministry of peer counseling which is effective, efficient, and a credit to the overall ministry of the church or organization will, in its operation, demonstrate all eight components.

1. A peer counseling program has the support of the leadership and/or staff of the church and the approval of the deacons, elders, and/or board members. This support should be active and specific in terms of roles, decision making, and accountability. Three areas of accountability that should be considered are: (1) doctrinal, (2) ethical or legal, and (3) financial.

Doctrinal accountability is the foundation for the program ministry related to the Christian mission of the sponsoring organization. The peer counseling program should have a clear statement of biblical teaching and principles that offer an integrated model of ministry.

27

Ethical or legal accountability is the framework of specific operational guidelines to ensure adherence to acceptable codes of conduct. The program should have a summary of rules and regulations that support basic human rights as well as the community laws for the provision of public helping services.

Financial accountability is the fiscal commitment of sources of income and a system of expenditures for the program ministry.

If after a full and careful review of the initial program proposal, the church organizational leadership supports peer counseling training, it must develop provisions for ongoing review and periodic evaluation by the church or parachurch ministry. The ultimate approval of the program should stipulate that any problems or controversies resulting from it should be negotiated between the church leadership and the peer counseling program people, without the threat of losing the program.

2. The peer counseling program has a designated program leader who directs, coordinates, and administers the service on behalf of the ministry.

- The leader may be a staff or lay person.
- He or she may be a professional, a paraprofessional, or a nonprofessional. The preference is, of course, for a professional program leader.
- A formal, written job description should be available.
- The service of the leader may be with or without compensation.
- He or she should have clear lines of accountability regarding implementation of policy, program development, program promotion, and reporting.

3. The peer counseling program has a defined *statement of mission* with ministry goals and a scope of service. The mission of the program represents the essential purpose(s) and the guiding philosophy for its existence. It is a succinct, yet broad statement about the program that should be available to the parent or host organization, the program staff, the counselors, and the general public. This statement will allow anybody to know the rationale for the program. The mission must be based on sound biblical principles and acceptable behavioral science knowledge that is consistent with the Bible. The mission of the program is *to show mercy* by being available to people in need. In the parable of the Good Samaritan (Luke 10:25–37), Jesus asks a young man, "Which of these three do you think was a neighbor to the man who fell into the hands of robbers?" He answers, "The one who had mercy on him." Jesus then tells him, "Go and do likewise." The mission of the program is also *to give service as unto the Lord.* In Matt. 25:31–40, Jesus states, "I tell you the truth, whatever you did for one of the least of these brothers you did for me." A third mission of the program is *to do good unto any and all people.* Paul urges us to do this in Gal. 6:10, where he writes, "As we have therefore opportunity, let us do good unto all men, especially unto them who are of the household of faith."

A statement of *organizational philosophy* shows the connection between the parent or host organization and the peer counseling program. It includes references to the charter or by-laws and describes the lines of accountability and the relationship of the program to the whole organization.

For any organization to be effective, it must have short-term and long-term goals. These goals should be reasonable, relevant, and linked to objectives that will give them a means for achievement.

The *scope of the program* may vary from one church or organization to another. However, it needs to be consistent within the specific church or organization. The *availability of counseling service* is related to the program's scope. The service should be available according to the designated facilities or service areas, such as offices or the counselor's home. An organization or church may not want its counselors to provide service outside the program building.

Scope should also address *compensation*. Counselors should be volunteers; their services are without salary or fee. No fee is required of counselees, but donations are accepted. Counselors do not receive any benefits, such as medical, dental, or life insurance. Peer counselors minister as a service to God and as an enrichment and spiritual growth for their own lives.

The *size of the program* will be determined by the number of program staff and counselors, facilities, and available resources, as well as by the amount of the budget. The number and type of people to be served in a primary and secondary area will make up the clientele. The *category of service to clientele* refers to the nonprofessional degree of specialization of services to be offered in the program. The counselors will be certified to work with people who have every-day problems of living, not mental illness. People who have severe personality disorders and major social problems should be referred to other more appropriate resources.

A *geographical area* should define the locality where the program services are to be extended in a primary or exclusive sense. It is prudent for the program to have a feasible service area to prioritize the services.

How much *time* should be given to the training? How many hours of service are required of the peer counselors? While these guidelines may be flexible, a minimum number of hours of training and service should be set. Fifty hours of training and two hours of service per week are the requirements used in some churches. Since the quality of the program is directly related to the preparation of the counselors, one should not underestimate the number of hours needed to prepare the trainees. If the trainees cannot commit to sufficient hours for training, they probably will not be able to commit to the necessary hours of service. If a person finds himself or herself unable to give the minimum amount of service time, another available person should be selected. A certified, commissioned peer counselor can serve from time to time, when it is convenient to their schedule.

Times of service may vary, but definite lengths should be written in the manual and understood by all those commissioned. A short service period is preferable to a lengthy one because even busy people usually will be able to commit to services of shorter duration. If the program guidelines permit it, a peer counselor may serve consecutive terms.

There are many categories of service. Although all the trainees will be trained with the same curriculum, some commissioned counselors will be better suited for certain counseling services. Specifically, there will be beginning and advanced counselors. Also, some counselors are more suited because of their personal experiences. For example, a counselor who has previously lost a spouse will often have a ready rapport with a counselee who is going through the same experience. In some churches and organizations, a list is made available with the names of the peer counselors, their level of training (beginning and advanced), and their special area of service; for example, Jane Brown—divorce; Mary Cook—death and dying; Tom Wallace—retirement. While commissioned counselors may have special interest areas, they may also have several areas of expertise in which they are capable of serving.

4. The peer counseling program has a dedicated group of trained and certified peer counselors of varying ages, ethnic backgrounds, and different life conditions (married, single, widowed, etc.). For peer counseling to be effective there must be a cross section of counselors. When a peer counseling program is just beginning in a church or organization, the program director may need to recruit different people representing each age group, ethnic background, socioeconomic

31

status, and life condition. After the program has been in operation for some time, the counselees usually tell their friends about the program, and in subsequent training classes there is a greater possibility for a cross section from which the program director can select.

5. The peer counseling program conducts a careful selection of counselors and implements an established course of training and an ongoing support structure for the counselors. Anyone may take the training, but only some will be selected to represent the ministry as commissioned peer counselors. The selection is made by the program director with the support of the pastor or organizational administrator. While each individual taking the training profits from what he or she has learned, not all individuals may be ready to become peer counselors when the training is completed. Most of those in this category will recognize their limitations themselves. Peer counseling training affects feelings and attitudes, and people taking the class will benefit from a better understanding of themselves and others. At a special public service, trainers are certified and commissioned by the sponsoring organization.

Training should be sequential and comprehensive, with various modalities of learning, including reading, listening to tapes, lectures, participation, observation, and role playing. Training should be theoretical or cognitive, affective, and value based. The most effective learning is accomplished with a variety of educational methods. It should be all encompassing in its approach to the trainee. Repetition of concepts, principles, and issues are important, as are relevant illustrations and examples. The evidence of training may be verified by rating sheets, tests, or practicums.

The training and support system should utilize church/ organizational resources as well as community volunteers. The program should have the most qualified and committed people available for training and supervision of the counselors. The selection of such people should be in concert with the ministry of mission objectives of the host organization so those who train, supervise, or consult are not working at cross-purposes with Christian peer counselors. The program director should maintain an active liaison to these community people and resources to ensure maximum referral possibilities and relevant training.

The training should be skills-oriented so a determination can be made as to whether the peer counselor has acquired the necessary competencies needed at each level before going on to the more advanced and rigorous training. Role-playing situations and simulations in class allow the program director or consultant to observe the trainee using the skills. Since this technique is used frequently in class, a number of observations may take place before a decision regarding competency is made. Some programs occasionally monitor and evaluate counselor performance by means of joint counseling or co-counseling arrangements. Selectively and with the counselee's consent, others use audio tapes to record counseling sessions for review at a later time.

Training should be ongoing after the peer counselor is commissioned. Once a peer counselor has been trained and is in service, the training should be continuous. Advanced classes can meet on a biweekly or monthly basis to continue to discuss their needs and concerns, hear resource people, and develop their skills. These meetings can be a support meeting for the counselors as well as a time for motivating and renewing their common bond.

A support structure should be in place for the commissioned counselors. Support may come by means of weekend retreats where they will be energized and motivated or by conferences where they will share ideas, concerns, and gain new knowledge and information. Attendance at community conferences should be arranged from time to time. Those who become overworked after an extended period of service may experience burn-out. Counselors should have access to professional consultation when it is needed. Finally, they should be able to share their personal growth as well as personal problems with the program director, the consultant, or a support group.

6. The peer counseling program has a policies/procedures manual which includes an approved budget, access to facilities and equipment, and a simple system of reporting. The manual should be short, concise, and informally bound (a loose-leaf notebook will do), but one must be readily available. It usually includes:

- Policies—general operating statements of philosophy and principle about the program
- Procedures—specific operating regulations and rules of the program
- Forms—a sample of each document used in the program
- Budget—an annual statement of itemized income and expenses
- System of reporting statistics—The number of certified peer counselors and the number of counselees seen during the year should be recorded. Names of counselees are not recorded, but categories of service (such as suicide, divorce, drug and alcohol abuse, etc.) are listed with appropriate numbers of counselees provided service.

7. The peer counseling program utilizes a professional counselor or helping professional who does regular training and serves as a consultant. The professional counselor will need to be available to the program for continued training consultation. This person may come from the Christian community or from the larger community. If a seminary or college is in the vicinity of the program, interns working toward advanced degrees may be used under the supervision of their mentors. The peer counseling program will gain respectability

and more cooperation from community people when there is a high regard for the professional counselor who trains and consults. Therefore, great care should be given to the selection of a counselor who is experienced and active in both the professional community and well known in the geographic area where the program is located. The professional counselor should have a job description and a clear line of accountability, primarily to the program director. In a secondary capacity, the consultant should be accessible to the board or other church organizational staff. Usually, a trainer or consultant receives a fee for services which constitutes a retainer. Some programs have this service donated by the professional counselor. A fee determination can be made by conferring with other not-for-profit organizations in the community, such as the Boys Clubs or Girl Scouts.

8. The peer counseling program is affiliated or networked with other peer counseling programs and paraprofessional service organizations to avoid isolation and to promote accountability. Often other programs provide supplemental training, referral sources, volunteer practicums, and supportive relationships among counselors. Every effort should be made to identify with the peer counseling movement on a regional or national basis. This includes subscriptions to peer counseling periodicals and attendance at educational conferences.

4

Developing and Maintaining a Peer Counseling Program

In the previous chapter, eight essential components were presented that should be characteristic of any peer counseling program. This chapter will focus on some primary considerations for establishing and maintaining a program.

Peer counseling, like every successful ministry or service, has organizational and functional structures. This chapter presents a summary of guidelines and "nuts and bolts" for the development and maintenance of a program based on the survey of programs listed in this book and the consulting experience of the authors.

THE DEVELOPMENT OF THE PROGRAM

Inspiration for the Program
Usually a peer counseling program comes into existence because of the strong interest and persistent efforts of one or two people. These individuals often are members of, or actively

identified with, the sponsoring organization. In most cases, the individuals are lay people, not staff or salaried employees. Their interest may arise from a personal experience of being helped by a professional, a community agency, or a friend. Many individuals get motivated by reading self-help books, attending seminars, or hearing about a successful care ministry from the media. Another impetus may be the individuals' awareness of the overwhelming needs of people within the organization and the lack of a relevant and readily available caring resource. Whatever the motivation, these inspired individuals want to duplicate a process or program of service to others. They eventually make a strong connection between basic helping and the uniqueness of Christian care giving. Ultimately these individuals envision this one-to-one helping as an organized peer counseling ministry.

The inspired person soon is sharing the idea of helping on a personal basis with other people in the organization such as a class, a group of friends, or a staff member. If the program idea does not originate from a staff, the individual is encouraged to do additional research on the idea.

A Plan for Peer Counseling

After gaining more information, and possibly encouragement from other people, the individual committed to the idea will need to enlist leadership support. Often he or she finds sympathy and general acceptance from a leader, but that leader often has some specific points of reservation and sees definite practical obstacles that preclude a quick adoption of the idea.

The leader may have problems with the idea due to theological issues, financial questions, legal matters, organizational duties, or concerns of ministry priority. These are realistic concerns for any leader, and for an idea to develop into a program, it must overcome these initial obstacles.

One of the best ways to deal with such obstacles is to formulate a ministry proposal. This proposal should answer the elements of the third component in the previous chapter, namely, a defined statement of mission with ministry goals and a scope of service. Another important part of the ministry proposal should focus on the first of the eight components, specifically, areas of financial, legal, and doctrinal accountability.

The initial ministry proposal is usually very provisional or sketchy. The proposal may be developed by the person seeking to establish the ministry, by a committee or task force, or by a person acting in the capacity of an advisor or consultant. This preliminary proposal often has to be endorsed by a corporate board, committee, or select group of leaders. Once the provisional endorsement is granted, a more comprehensive program must be developed.

There is more than one way to develop a quality peer counseling program. Three general development strategies are being used by Christian organizations. The most common approaches are: (1) a unique, original, locally developed program, (2) a consultant-developed program, and (3) a "packaged" program model.

A uniquely developed local program results from the creativity and special innovation of the organization which sponsors the program. This model can be informal in its structure or highly developed. It may be the creation of one outstanding person who has charismatic leadership and care-giving abilities. It may be the result of a care-giving team of individuals who have collective leadership and group ownership of the program. The curriculum and training material can be an eclectic integration of several helping approaches. It may be closely identified with the pastoral care ministry of the church, or it may be a separate, more distinct ministry identified with a church counseling program. In some cases it may be the primary method by which a church organizes its membership care.

A consultant-developed program is designed for the organization by an outside specialist. The consultant provides a program proposal, a plan for implementation, and resources for its on-going operation. This peer counseling specialist may work by contract or agreement, with or without compensation. The program may be the outcome of his primarily solo activity, or it may be mediated through a committee or task force. Nonetheless, a distinctive feature of this strategy is that the organization gives the specialist an expert role in the formulation and operation of the program. The consultant may continue with the organization after the program is developed, or he or she may terminate involvement at a certain place in time to return, as needed, for evaluation or special assistance.

A packaged program is a preexisting model of service adopted as a whole by the organization. Often these packaged programs are the result of a well-known counseling leader or an established counseling training center. This mode of development usually requires organizational leaders and potential peer counselors to be trained at regional or national conferences with a manual of knowledge and skills, augmented by audio and video tapes. These packaged programs charge a fee for the initial enrollment, training, and ongoing affiliation. Often, the organization becomes identified as a locally endorsed or certified affiliate of the service provider. An example of such a program is the Stephen Ministries.

The Operation of the Program

The operation of a program formally begins when leaders in authority accept a ministry plan that has been developed from one of the strategies mentioned above. The following are associated with the start of the program: (1) selection of the director, (2) establishment of a governing or advising board, (3) allocation of physical facilities for clerical use and counseling appointments, (4) commitment to a program budget, (5) formation of an operating manual, (6) recruitment of trainees, (7) initiation of program publicity, (8) acquisition of program resources such as training materials, (9) scheduling of peer counseling classes, and (10) commitment to prayer.

1. Selection of a program director. A peer counseling director is basic to the smooth and effective operation of a program. The first task of leadership for the organization is to recruit or appoint a director. This person is given a job description by leadership and is accountable to an advisory or governing board or committee. If there is a professional director of counseling for the organization, the program director may be under the administrative supervision of this professional. In some cases, the pastor of the church may have administrative and supervisory oversight of the director. When this position has been filled, the new director is then primarily responsible for the start-up of the other eight steps of the program.

After an interval of service, the organizational leadership should conduct a formal evaluation of the director. A ninety-day evaluation is appropriate, followed by one yearly. Should the director's performance prove unsatisfactory, the organizational leadership will need to find a replacement. Program development should be delayed or temporarily suspended during months of start-up if a competent director is not available. The leadership of the organization must have full confidence in the person who is designated as the director.

2. *Governing or advisory board/committee.* Initially, not all programs have a group of individuals who have corporate responsibility for the program—often with new programs, only one or two individuals serve in this capacity. Ideally, a more diverse group of people will evolve.

The members of this group may come from a variety of professions; they may be mental health practitioners, health care specialists, lawyers, accountants, teachers, or clergy. A central responsibility of this leadership group is to support and advise the director and to lend corporate sanction to the program.

3. *Allocation of physical facilities.* The peer counseling program should have a designated area of physical space and facility use. Ideally, it will have its own counseling offices which are private, comfortable, and accessible. There should be room for storage of program materials and locked files for

records and forms. Many programs find it useful to have a clerical person to answer the telephone during regular hours and a telephone-answering service as a backup. Adequate spaces for peer counseling classes and support group meetings should be available.

4. *Program budget.* A simple, functional budget should be established with line items of income and expense. Most programs can start with a volunteer director but may need a small retainer to hire a consultant.

The major cost of a new program is related to the purchase of training materials, the formulation of a manual with program forms, and reference books relating to peer counseling. A $500 start-up budget is adequate. If a packaged program is adopted, the cost for enrollment, training, and affiliation alone could be several thousands of dollars.

A good policy regarding fixed expenses, initially and thereafter, is to seek a volunteer and noncompensatory staff, including the director, resource training people, and consultant.

The income for the program is usually a subsidy from the organization as an investment in ministry. However, provisions should be made for donations to the program by those being helped. Fund-raising activities also bring contributions into the program.

Even with good stewardship practices and active solicitation of income, a peer counseling program will need to be partially supported by the sponsoring organization.

5. *Operating manual.* Every effort should be made to have a manual for the peer counseling program. Initially, it may include only a statement of mission, an organizational chart, job descriptions, a rudimentary budget, and some program forms. Most programs start small with a basic manual that is made more comprehensive as the program develops. Indeed, all programs have manual revisions on a regular basis, which result in their developing greater sophistication with the years of operation.

The director has a primary responsibility for the development of the manual, while the corporate leadership approves its content on a periodic basis.

6. *Recruitment of trainees.* The organization should have an open policy to its constituency for the peer counseling training. The director will solicit involvement also to individuals known to be talented in the care giving ministry. Recruitment announcements should be made as widely as possible, using a variety of media. Those expected to attend the beginning class will complete an enrollment form that provides basic identifying information. Preferably, the director will make a contract in person or by the telephone with each enrollee before the first scheduled meeting of the beginning class.

7. *Program publicity.* Depending on the size of the organization, the mode and type of publicity may vary. However, the outcome should be the same—the people should be aware of the program! Everyone associated with it should have a clear understanding of who may be served, who provides the help, and where to make the contact for services.

For any organization, the most natural, inexpensive, and effective publicity is word-of-mouth. Person to person promotion is done by the organizational leaders, program director, and perspective peer counselors in the form of announcements to groups, classes, and meetings of the entire membership.

The written word is another form of publicity which can be used. It may be only a one-page, typed summary of information about the ministry, or it may be something more sophisticated. Some programs use a professionally printed brochure which includes the name, auspices, and location of the service center as well as a statement of purpose and the nature of help to be provided.

The organization may have access to a larger promotional market by use of a community newspaper. Radio and television offer an even broader scope of publicity.

After the program is operating, the people who are helped

will, undoubtedly, spread the word to others. Indeed, those served may become peer counselors themselves and continue to promote the ministry by their own service.

8. *The acquisition of program resources.* The director, with the approval of the leadership, will make a selection from a survey of available and relevant training material. This material may be handbooks from established programs, general peer counseling manuals, or counseling reference books. Some programs begin with a purchase of audio cassettes and videotapes. The investment may be small and additions made as the program evolves.

9. *Scheduling of classes.* A calendar of the beginning dates and times needs to be established by the director. Care should be given to make allowances for family and work schedules as well as those of any existing ministry and service programs.

Weekly and biweekly meetings seem best for most organizations. Night or weekend classes are usually the preferred time options. When the actual scheduling varies, it is important to have ample advance notice for enrollment, although consistency of meeting times and places is preferred. Most active people interested in peer counseling cannot commit to more than three hours a week.

10. *Commitment to prayer.* All service done in the name of Jesus and for the extension of the kingdom of God is supported by prayer. The organizational leaders and director need to pray regularly for the program both as a group and individually. There should be periodic solicitations of prayer from other groups and classes in the church or paraprofessional organization.

THE MAINTENANCE OF THE PROGRAM

Selection of Counselors for Certification
A formal procedure must be in place to select counselors from those trainees completing the beginning and advanced classes.

Each trainee will have prior knowledge of the criteria and procedures for the selection.

An important qualification for a peer counselor is the possession of any spiritual gifts of the Holy Spirit related to caring ministries. A general list of the spiritual gifts is found in Romans 12, 1 Corinthians 12, and Ephesians 4. Those particular to caring ministries include the gifts of exhortation, knowledge, discernment, mercy, healing, and helps. A simple assessment guide to spiritual gifts is the Wagner-Modified Houts Questionnaire (revised edition, 1985), available from the Charles E. Fuller Institute in Pasadena, California.

A fundamental requirement for all programs is a completed application form with a statement of Christian faith and an interview with the program director. Personal references should be included in the application. When there are certified peer counselors in the program, a group interview can supplement the interview by the program director.

To assist in the selection, some programs have a stated criteria of personal qualities and a verification of skill levels by role playing or case presentations. The use of psychological tests such as the Minnesota Multiphasic Personality Inventory also may be used.

Certification and Commissioning of Counselors

The peer counseling program becomes more official and formal by means of certification and commissioning. The program has both structure and validity when every beginning and advanced peer counselor receives a certificate in recognition of their level of training.

The program director recommends a trainee to the organizational leaders for acknowledgment of completed training and eligibility for certification. The certificate is prepared with the name of the trainee, level of training (beginning or advanced), date of issuance, and signature of the program director and possibly a corporate leader of the organization.

With a list of eligible trainees, the organization periodically schedules a commissioning service to grant certificates in a public meeting. The purposes of the commissioning are (1) recognition of peer counseling as a Christian ministry, (2) validation of the training for the counselor, (3) identification of the counselor with the sponsoring organization, and (4) collective ownership of those attending the commissioning and by the constituency of the organization. Ideally, the commissioning should have an order of service to include a presentation of the program, introduction of the trainees, presentation of certificates, and a time of dedicatory prayer. Some organizations require the certified counselor to sign a covenant of commitment following the commissioning service. A list of commissioned peer counselors is maintained by the organization.

Continued Training of Counselors

All certified counselors who are assigned people to help by the program director should be committed to ongoing training. The organization should schedule this training on a regular basis. The training may review basic concepts and consolidate the skill development of the counselor. The counselor will need to confidentially share experiences from peer counseling. By written consent of the counselees, some programs may use verbatim case examples and audio tapes from counseling sessions.

Continued training is needed in the use of counseling forms and recording responsibilities. All counselors should be aware of changes in the content of the operating manual. Beginning counselors will get advanced training, and some of them will become certified as advanced counselors.

Besides regular and periodic training meetings, every counselor serving people at the organization should have individual supervision from the program director or another professional helping person. From time to time, the program consultant can be used for either individual or group supervision. With consent of the counselee, the program director or the consultant can be a participant observer in the counseling sessions.

Support of Counselors

Due to the demands of active peer counseling, the program should provide for a support system to all counselors. The support can be periodic rotation of the counselor from active weekly counseling assignments to a time of inactivity for rest and renewal. A semiannual or annual retreat for program staff and counselors is definitely a major part of a support system. The assigning of each counselor to another counselor in a "buddy system" offers fellowship and friendship support. Support can be given by the provision of peer and/or professional counseling to the commissioned counselor.

Reporting of Service

The sponsoring organization has a responsibility to keep its constituency up to date on the ministry of peer counseling. Therefore, regularly prepared reports and oral presentations will be made to governing board/committees and at public gatherings. From time to time an anonymous vignette regarding the services of a peer counselor or help received by a counselee may be shared in an organizational newsletter or other media. It is beneficial for the peer counselor to give testimony of his or her ministry to the organization. Lastly, many organizations require an annual report from the program director.

Integration into the Church or Organization

Peer counseling should not be an isolated program but rather an integral part of the total life of the church or organization. This involvement is necessary so that it will receive and give support and enhance positive communication about the ministry.

The program director and the peer counselors should be active in building organizational esprit de corps. This spirit should include team building with other ministries. Every effort should be made to have a unified mission and a common expression of community.

Networking to the Community

The program director and the consultant are the primary people responsible for maintaining a good connection to community professionals and agencies. The goal is for the community at large to endorse and fully utilize the peer counseling ministry. Furthermore, the program should interface with community resources to a maximum degree for information and referral as well as training.

Recruiting the Counselors

There should be a plan for the periodic recruitment of new counselors to expand services, replace those who are no longer active, and service special needs. Current and former peer counselors are often very helpful in recruiting.

In maintaining a program, recruitment may become more difficult because the most obvious prospects are already serving. On the other hand, recruiting may become easier because it has gained a favorable reputation and is "the" place for an innovative ministry.

The peer counseling staff and counselors should be careful that they do not give the impression that their bonding and peer culture is closed and unreceptive to new trainees.

Other church or organizational leaders also need to be a part of the recruitment team. The pastoral staff or executive director usually has contact with those seeking a place of service. With these leaders serving as recruiters, the optimum staffing for the program is better ensured.

Promotion of the Program

A continued effort of program promotion and linkage by the program director and peer counselors is essential. This is accomplished by use of the same methods which were used in establishing the program, but more specific strategies should be planned to enlist cooperation, locate income sources, and overcome known resistances to the program.

Evaluation

Various levels of evaluation are necessary for an ongoing, viable program. On any level, surveys and sample feedback forms provide relevant data to measure a program's effectiveness. The most obvious survey would be directed to the counselees by means of an anonymous consumer questionnaire. Peer counselors themselves should be surveyed as to their insights and ideas. Also important is input from the general constituency. Finally, the community from which the program operates may be sampled to determine the impact of services.

Something else to consider is an outside evaluation by another peer counseling team or consultant. The information accumulated by outside people may be more objective and rigorous.

A director should make sure a periodic evaluation is completed, even if it is not requested or required. This process is necessary because the nontraditional nature of the ministry may cause questions to be raised that need to be answered. In this respect, the evaluation is proactive and useful in advocating the program.

5

Training and the Peer Counseling Class

The previous chapters have provided background for a complete peer counseling program, and now we will turn our attention to the peer counseling class. The tone that is set the first time the class assembles is of the utmost importance. Whether this class will be a dull class of learning theory and skills presented in a cut-and-dried way or whether it will be an exciting, unforgettable experience of new awareness and growth will, to a large extent, depend on the leader. He or she must be secure enough within himself or herself to step back and allow the trainees to claim ownership of their own class. The trainees must be empowered to become the best counselors they are capable of becoming.

This chapter addresses the format and substance of the class. The class will include multiple meetings, with the exact number to be determined by each program. Most programs will have two categories of classes, the *beginning* class and the *advanced* class. The beginning class will consist of at least thirty hours of training prior to the certification. The advanced class can be of a more limited duration; for example, six meetings related to suicidal counseling and another sequence of meetings related to more advanced skill development. The advanced class also can be a series of knowledge and skill-building classes that certify the person as an advanced peer counselor. It is implicit in the program training that some will be beginning peer counselors, others will be beginners with advanced training, and a select group will be certified advanced peer counselors.

Throughout the country there is a wide variety of training programs with diverse curricula, methods of teaching, modes of supervision, and types of practicums. A well-designed and efficiently operated Christian peer counseling program provides training in the essential values, knowledge, and basic skills any trainee should possess before certification as a peer counselor.

This chapter and the following one will present the areas of training for a beginning and advanced class. While these chapters are not a training manual, they do provide an overview of a program. Trainers are encouraged to use their own creativity in the actual sequence of the curriculum; thus, the chapters recommend a variety of resources for use in training. These additional resources offer the classes comprehensive and indepth exposure to more specialized or technical areas.

THE BEGINNING PEER COUNSELING CLASS

Trainees in the beginner class need to be told at the first class meeting what a peer counselor is and what his or her role will be. Some trainees may have a different conception than others in the class about the program. The leader will want to make certain that everyone understands the operational definition of a peer counselor and what the expectations will be of the training class.

What is *Peer Counseling?*

Peer counseling is a mode of interpersonal sharing in which a trained person provides help and support to one or

50

more individuals. Broadly, peer counseling is purposeful caring and sharing between two people whereby individuals are helped with the everyday problems of life. In the limited definition, peer counseling is the exchange of helpful communication from one person to another. Listening and talking on a one-to-one basis is common to all peer counseling approaches.

Peer counseling is empathic, paraprofessional communication that involves knowledge and skills often used by professional therapists. The peer counselor uses generic and scientifically validated helping skills that degreed and licensed counselors have made systematic through practice, research, and scholarly publications.

The art of communicating between a helper and a helpee is essentially the same for both the professional and the peer counselor. Peer counseling benefits much from the legacy of approaches, methods, modalities, and techniques that are generally accepted as a part of the therapeutic or healing communication between people. Therefore, the peer counseling movement represents one important extension of the field of professional counseling.

The major characteristics that distinguish peer counseling from professional counseling are as follows: peer counseling is more natural and less formal; it is more accessible because it is indigenous; it does not involve financial obligation, fees, or restrictions; and it fosters a sense of mutual exchange because both the helper and the helpee regard each other as equals.

What is a *Peer Counselor?*

A peer counselor is one who has been trained in communication skills for the purpose of helping another person or peer with personal or social problems.

A peer counselor is a person who cares about others and takes time to listen to their problems. Without giving advice, the peer counselor assists the person in managing or solving his or her own problems. By using active listening counseling skills, the peer counselor helps counselees clarify their values, express their feelings, and explore the appropriate, available solutions.

While a goal of the class may be to teach basic counseling skills to beginning trainees, an equally important goal is to develop positive attitudes toward helping others. This goal can be accomplished only if the peer counseling trainer has established an atmosphere where trainees learn to respect themselves and each other. For this to happen, the trainer must model a positive regard toward others and their interactions. Peer counseling leaders must not allow trainees to be disrespectful or to "put down" other trainees or themselves.

Trainers who teach peer counseling must be willing to encourage trainees to initiate interactions with other trainees who may need their help. This should be encouraged at each meeting, so while trainees are learning counseling skills, they are also developing an awareness of situations where their skills may be used.

As the class progresses and trust is built, a feeling of unity permeates the group. Peer counselors have described this feeling in terms like, "We are a family," or, "We are bonded together." Because of this feeling, a support system for each member of the class is put into place. No one feels alone! And no matter what happens to a member of the group, that person knows that he has friends who will listen and be supportive.

What is *Christian Peer Counseling?*

Christian peer counseling is support and assistance given by a Christian, in service to Jesus Christ, to another person in need. The primary focus is on truthful and empathic communication along with appropriate use of spiritual resources such as prayer and the Bible.

Given the relatively new development of peer counseling in the Christian community, the authors of this book recognize there is no consensus as to a description of what constitutes "Christian peer counseling." However, there is widespread acceptance of the fact that Christian laity do minister to others as disciples of Jesus Christ. This ministry of outreach to others is motivated by obedience to the great commission (Matt. 28:18–20) and the great commandments (Mark 12:29–31).

Service to others on a one-to-one basis by Christian non-professionals has many designations. Among the identities used in the Christian community are lay caregivers, lay counselors, friendship counselors, lay pastoral counselors, lay shepherds, people helpers, and discipleship counselors.

The Christian ministry models for nonprofessional counseling are diverse in philosophy, motivation, and method. Some well-known models are organized as an instructional and confrontational approach to sin or wrong doing, with the Bible as the source of knowledge about healthy living. Other models are organized as helping and healing approaches to dysfunctional living, with an integrated system of scriptural truths and behavioral science knowledge.

The Christian peer counselor should be trained in all helping skills and techniques that are not inconsistent with the values and virtues of Christ-like living. Christian peer counseling is directed to the whole person seeking to reconcile an individual to himself, others, and God. The Christian peer counselor has a reliance on the Holy Spirit for divine wisdom, power, and love. Christian peer counseling is committed to the efficacy of such distinctive methods as corporate worship, fellowship, Scripture memorization, meditation, fasting, inner healing, intercessory prayer, confession of sin, repentance, and forgiveness.

The training classes and ongoing supervision of the program should equip every peer counselor for a ministry of service that fully employs all the resources of the Christian community according to the need and self-determination of the counselees.

RESPONSIBILITIES OF COUNSELORS

Confidentiality
The unity that is felt in class comes about because of trust, and a vital incentive to trust is the confidentiality honored among

class members. Clear ground rules must be established at the beginning of the class, so trainees know they are not to share or discuss information about people's personal or family lives outside of the classroom. To show the importance of confidentiality and to witness to a consensus among the members, the program can have a written covenant of confidentiality. The trainees will feel safe discussing their personal problems in class only if they are assured that the confidentiality rule is never broken.

If, for any reason, confidentiality is broken, the situation should be discussed openly in class, with each person having the opportunity to express his or her feelings. If confidentiality is broken twice by the same person, consideration should be given to the fact that this person may not be suitable as a peer counselor, and withdrawal from the class may definitely be indicated.

Professional and Legal Issues

In the beginning class, the trainees need to know the distinction between paraprofessional and professional counselors. There should be a presentation of the levels of training, certification, and laws governing different types of counselors. Furthermore, the trainees should thoroughly understand the legal philosophies and statutes related to professional counseling in the state where the program operates. Additional training, with examples, should be given concerning the liabilities of a peer counseling program. Cautions and limitations of a peer counselor should be highlighted. The importance of supervision and the importance of referrals to appropriate sources of help and a strict adherence to program policy should be emphasized.

Expectations of Service

The number of hours required of the peer counselor may vary at each church or organization, but whatever the requirement is, the trainee should be aware of the requirement and in agreement with it. If the number of service hours required is too large, the program may soon suffer. Peer counselors sometimes drop out of the program if they feel they cannot keep up with the expectations. While a minimum number of hours of service may be set, the peer counselor may exceed this number if she or he desires, with advisement from the program director.

Because peer counselors have a real desire to help, they may feel that they have failed if the counselee's problems are not being managed well or resolved. A discussion on "not feeling guilty" is important to have. The peer counselor must realize that all situations will not come to a happy conclusion. Sometimes, the person needing help should be referred to a professional, and the peer counselor in this situation will act only as a bridge to the therapist or another helping person.

THE RELATIONSHIP BETWEEN THE COUNSELOR AND THE COUNSELEE

Who to Counsel

People are seen by peer counselors when their needs relate to personal problems (drug or alcohol abuse, grief, divorce), vocational problems (retirement, lay-offs, strikes), relational problems (marital discord, parental conflicts, coworkers' disputes), or other everyday problems of living. Although the program does offer supportive counseling to assist anyone in need, it is important to note that the services cannot be represented as a social agency or mental health clinic. People with serious physical problems, mental disorders, emotional disturbances, economic destitution, or social maladjustment should be referred to the most appropriate resource. The program should complement professional or speciality care.

Counselees at Risk

A brief presentation and discussion of personal problems should be included in the curriculum. Training categories might include domestic violence, drug and alcohol abuse, suicide, life-threatening illnesses, death and dying, divorce and remarriage, step-families, teenage pregnancy, conflicts at work, retirement, and any other problems commonly experienced by the community. The advanced class will study these problems in depth, and the beginning peer counselors should have at least a working awareness of the signs and systems of personal adversities so that they can recognize and quickly access them and provide the appropriate services for the counselees.

Referral and Networking to Resources

The knowledge of how and when to refer the counselee is basic to training a peer counselor. The beginning class should have a thorough familiarity of the variety of helping resources in the community. These include the various professionals and the specialized agencies. The means and methods for making a referral should be presented to the class. The ability to deal with the reservations and initial resistance of the counselee is an important part of this process. Each trainee needs to know about the use of a resource directory and have some working knowledge of eligibility requirements for the services. Trainees will receive more lasting benefit by learning through personal research. They may do this by taking individual assignments and investigating various helping professions and specific agencies.

CURRICULUM FOR THE BEGINNING CLASS

Building Social Ease and Self-Awareness

Before a peer counselor can feel confident in helping someone, he or she must be at ease with that person. People who may make wonderful counselors sometimes feel inadequate or timid when talking to a stranger. Exercises to overcome these feelings are important to have in class.

Some general guidelines for class discussion are outlined below.

1. Introduce yourself to the stranger by giving him or her your name. The stranger will normally respond by stating his or her name. If this does not happen, it is permissible to ask for the name.

2. Listen to how the person responds. He may be very ill-at-ease when talking to strangers himself, so watch his body language. If he gives only his name without volunteering further information, notice any objects he or she is wearing, such as an antique broach or athletic shirt. After the initial introductions, an opening remark might be, "What a lovely broach. Is it a family heirloom?" The person then may feel more comfortable talking about what she knows, in this case, her family. If it is not a family heirloom, she will probably volunteer, "No, it is just something that I purchased at Macy's (or Bullock's or a favorite store)." This invites more conversation about the joys or perils of shopping. If someone has on a Dodgers, Celtics, or Forty-Niners t-shirt, a natural opener would be, "How's the team doing this year?" Most people are happy to talk about their favorite team.

3. Use information that the person gives to continue the conversation. For example, the counselee may say, "No, the broach isn't a family heirloom. I bought it on my trip to Germany." She has just given you the information that she has made a trip abroad, and she probably would enjoy talking about it.

4. Avoid asking questions that can be answered with just a yes or no. Feelings cannot be expressed in one word, so it is very appropriate to ask, "How did you feel about . . . ?"

5. Show sincerity and respect to the stranger. Let him know that you are truly interested and care about what he has to say. Also, put him at ease by not asking private questions that would cause him to put his guard up and become defensive.

After the suggestions listed above have been discussed, the leader may divide the group into dyads. If two people already know each other, make sure they exchange partners with someone else. Give the pairs ten minutes to get to know each other by practicing what they have just learned. After the ten-minute time period has elapsed, have each member of the group introduce his new "friend" by name and tell something about him. The people in the group are not only getting to practice meeting a stranger, they also are getting to know everyone in the class.

The group may then be divided in subgroups according to birthday months, their states of birth, or their favorite colors. After introductions are made, have each person see what else he or she has in common with others in the group.

When these orientation activities have been completed, bring the class back together and ask each one to share how he or she felt when another person was being introduced and how that person felt when he was the one initiating the conversation. Allow the members of the class to talk about the things they found the most difficult and the most rewarding.

During the time of expressing concerns about meeting strangers, someone will probably mention, "I can talk to people who are 'like me,' but I don't know how to relate to people who are 'different.'" The ways people are different should be discussed, with special emphasis being placed on the fact that people may be more interesting because they are not like others. If someone speaks with an accent, that person may have very interesting information to share about the country, or region of the country, where he or she was born. Or, if a person appears to be less educated, he or she may be talented in other areas and can tell the group about skills of which they have no knowledge. The group should come to realize, if they have not done so already, that there are no people "better" than other people. Being different does not make a person better, nor does it make one worse. Before a person can become an effective peer counselor, he or she must learn to be accepting and tolerant of all people and not be "turned-off" by someone who is different.

Someone in the class may say that he can talk to anyone when it is one-on-one, but that a group of strangers in a room "scares him to death." The leader can point out that while numbers may be somewhat intimidating, the thing to remember is that each person in the room is an individual. Usually, there are some people standing or sitting alone, and it is easier to make introductions with one of them on a one-on-one basis than it is to approach a large group. Reassure the class that practice is the key that makes the new situations become easier and easier. Persistence and not becoming discouraged are others.

Another approach to personal understanding and rapport is for each class member to share something about his or her own life. This personal sharing can follow a suggested outline that asks each trainee to tell his or her name, age, family of origin, and perhaps about a positive or traumatic childhood experience, an outstanding life achievement, or a favorite personal possession. The personal sharing may be open-ended, with each class member sharing according to his or her own comfort level.

Guidelines for Counseling Peers

Be nonjudgmental. If a person is to be an effective peer counselor, he or she must be open and accepting of all people. Preconceived ideas or stereotyping must be avoided. One of the most important rules in the class is that there are no "put downs." Because it is important for trainees to learn to share their own feelings in order to help the others they are counseling to do the same thing, they must feel comfortable in class and not be afraid of someone putting them down for expressing their true feelings. When members of the class observe the "no put down" rule, a level of ease and trust develops in the class.

Be empathic. Trainees need to try to put themselves in

the other person's place so they can see his or her point of view. To empathize is to feel "with" that person; to sympathize is to feel "for" him or her; and to conform is to feel "like" that person. Trainees may never perfectly understand people, but they can imagine what the person is feeling.

Deal with the feelings first. Helping a person solve a problem is often easy. The hard part is to help him or her deal with the feelings associated with that problem. Listen for words that express feelings and explore them. It is important to help the class members distinguish a variety of feelings and to develop a language for the vocabulary of feelings.

Listen between the lines. This is sometimes referred to as listening with the "third ear." A problem that is presented first may not be the primary one, and by listening to what is being said (and what is not being said) a peer counselor may uncover more essential aspects of the problem.

Do not argue, either verbally or nonverbally. When a peer counselor is trying to understand the other person, it is a handicap to argue mentally while he or she is listening. Arguing sets up a barrier between the peer counselor and the counselee and includes body language that communicates either disapproval or indifference.

Stick with the here and now. Get rid of any distractions; the counselee deserves the peer counselor's undivided attention. Actively focus on the words, the ideas, and the feelings related to the subject. This rule reinforces the importance of proper listening skills.

Do not take responsibility for the other person's problem. While the peer counselor may empathize with the counselee, he or she does not assume responsibility for the problem. An effective counselor will enable the counselee to "have ownership" of his own problems and to make realistic life adjustments for himself.

Do not be an "advice giver." This is one of the main rules for a peer counselor. Where specific directions or instructions are necessary, the counselor should be certain not to give premature or excessive advice. Most trainees find it difficult in the beginning to abide by this rule because it is something they have probably been doing for a long period of time. However, by understanding that advice is not the solution for most problems, the peer counselor soon learns how much more effective allowing the counselee to work out his or her own solutions is. The emphasis here is upon personal problem solving and decision making. Furthermore, this rule promotes self-help that often comes through trial and error.

Keep confidentiality. Each counselor develops a strong commitment to the dignity and privacy of every person he or she helps in a peer counseling context. The counselor explicitly shares with the counselee the fact that all information about his or her personal and family life will be held in confidence, except those prescribed areas of information that the counselor is required by mandate to share with the program director or authorities.

Be genuine and sincere. The spirit and the attitude that the counselor conveys to those receiving assistance should represent a genuine willingness to help and a true interest in the person's well-being. Furthermore, the counselor has to do his or her best to provide help with all the capabilities the counselor possesses and without any desire to harm or hurt the counselee.

Be a vital part of a caring network. The counselor should convey by word and deed a context of community and esprit de corps with the caring program and the host church or organization. Every effort should be made to avoid a "lone ranger" mentality when providing help. The counselee should know there are other complimentary resources available from the program and in the community of which he or she is a vital part. In short, individual peer counseling is a natural extension of a caring or healing community and should be presented as such to the counselee.

Five Core Counseling Skill Areas

Prior to certification, a beginning peer counselor must have mastery in five core skills (presented below): (1) active listening, (2) sending effective messages, (3) problem solving and decision making, (4) clarifying conflicts and finding resolutions, and (5) intervening in a crisis.

Active listening skills. The following is a checklist of the characteristics of active listening:

1. Be attentive and look interested.

2. Put yourself in the other's place to understand what the person is saying (content) and how he or she feels (emotion) and the meaning of the situation (values).

3. Convey understanding and acceptance through non-verbal behavior (voice tone, posture, facial expression, eye contact, and gestures).

4. Restate the person's most important thoughts and feelings.

5. Do not interrupt, offer advice or suggestions, or bring up similar feelings and problems from one's own experience.

6. Do not argue mentally with yourself (i.e., self-talk).

7. Do not antagonize the speaker with hasty judgments.

8. Have a desire to listen. Someone has said there are no uninteresting people—only disinterested listeners!

9. React appropriately. Applaud with nods, smiles, comments, and encouragements.

10. Develop an attitude that listening is fun and personally enriching.

Sometimes a human being has an emotional need to talk as an outlet for stored up thoughts about problems or good news. A person in this mood does not want to be challenged, judged, advised, debated, interrupted, or sidetracked into a maze of detail. The person is saying, "Please listen to me. I need to share my thoughts and feelings. I need to understand myself. For that I need your patience and tolerance, for I may not be logical, clear, or correct. But wait until I've expressed myself completely before you point this out to me."

According to Lyman K. Steil, an educator and authority on listening, "Eight major studies conducted over a period of fifty years with a diverse subject population have resulted in the unchallenged conclusion that listening is the primary communication activity utilized daily by the average individual. Without question, listening has been found to be central to the personal, social, educational and professional success of every individual." It is recognized in the communication field that the average adult gains an estimated 90 percent of his information just from listening.

In the beginning peer counseling class, the trainees must understand the importance of listening to others and must be willing to work diligently until the skill becomes very natural to them. To help them remember the significance of their job, a simple, paper bookmark may be given to them with Elton Mayo's words on it, "One friend, one person who is truly understanding, who takes the trouble to listen to us as we consider our problems, can change our whole outlook on the world."

When ordinary listening is used, friends share thoughts, experiences, and feelings. Each person presents and compares life events while pursuing his or her own line of thought. In contrast to this, peer counselors who use active listening encourage their counselees to keep the focus on themselves.

Role playing is a very useful technique for teaching active listening skills. Two people may take their chairs to the center of the circle, with one assuming the role of the counselor and the other that of the counselee. The remaining trainees in the circle observe body language, reflective listening, questioning, and closure. At the end of the exercise, the trainees sitting in the circle give feedback to the role players. Each trainee in the circle should be allowed to take his or her turn being either the counselor or the counselee.

In some peer counseling training programs, the trainers prepare active listening ratings sheets to rate role-playing situations.

Sending effective messages. Effective messages are those which are most likely to be heard and understood by people who receive them. Five components for sending effective messages are presented below:

- The verbal and nonverbal message must be congruent. If the words spoken say that the person is feeling fine, but the person frowns, an incongruent message is being sent. This kind of communication is often confusing because the person receiving the message must decide whether to pay attention to the verbal or the nonverbal message.

- One must "own" responsibility for feelings and actions. At any moment in time people are individually in charge of their own feelings, and even though they sometimes cannot control how they feel, they do have responsibility for how they express their feelings.

- Personal feelings are best expressed by using "I" statements. One must use his or her own feelings about the person who will receive the message. For example, the speaker may say, "I am angry with you . . . ", instead of saying, "you make me angry when you . . . ."

- Care for and acceptance of the receiver's feelings and reactions to the message must be communicated. Active listening may be used to respond to the receiver's reactions. For example, one might say, "I hear you saying you are confused," or, "What I hear you saying is . . . ."

- Speakers must convey explicit expectations in their messages as to what they want the other person to change. If this is not done, the receiver of the message may perpetuate his or her personal dilemma, believing he or she is powerless to resolve the situation.

Three kinds of questions are used to communicate effective messages. These are *closed* questions, *open-ended* questions, and *why* questions. Closed questions ask for specific information such as, "Did you go to the library?" The person usually answers with a one-word answer, either yes or no. This type of question discourages the person from talking. Closed questions usually begin with "is," "did," or "have." Open-ended questions encourage conversation because feelings are allowed to be discussed. The most effective questions usually begin with "how" or "what." An example of this kind of question is, "How do you feel about the dance?" Why questions should be used infrequently because they often put the receiver on the defensive. Sometimes "why" questions make people feel they must explain or justify what has happened.

Practicing problem solving and decision making. Four steps are generally recognized in effective problem solving and decision making:

- Define the problem and identify the decision. Sometimes the first problem revealed is not the primary one. More conversation is often needed to get to the root of the problem.
- List all possible alternatives and identify choices of action. Some people with problems may feel they have no alternative, so it is important to brainstorm and consider all the possibilities.
- Evaluate the alternatives by exploring each one individually and prioritizing them. Personal values should be considered before a decision can be made. Some of the alternatives may conflict with a person's values, and those may be discarded. After looking at all of the pros and cons and seeing that all the information has been

gathered, the choice of which is the best alternative may be made.

- Make an action plan and followup on the outcome. After the action plan is carried out, see if the problems are corrected. If a workable solution has not been achieved, another alternative may be selected. Take into consideration all consequences resulting from the plan.

People make decisions every day on the basis of tradition, authority, values, or impulse. When a family decides to buy a live tree for Christmas rather than an artificial one, that decision may be based on the fact that they have always had a live tree. Buying an artificial tree would break a family tradition. When a middle-aged executive chooses to change his diet because a respected medical journal links red meat to heart disease, he is making an authority-based decision. When a teenager decides not to get drunk at a party, he or she is making a value-based decision because he or she has personal convictions (based on values) against drinking. When someone relies on "plastic" money to satisfy a spur-of-the-moment want, regardless of financial dilemmas, he or she is making an impulse-based decision.

The technique of role playing may again be used to teach decision making in the class. The counselee may have a decision to make, and the trainee may help that person by using the steps of decision making. The entire class may participate by watching the role-playing situation and giving feedback at the end.

Clarifying conflicts and finding resolutions. Conflict may be defined as a disagreement, dispute, or quarrel of any duration. Conflicts are inevitable in life because of differences that polarize, if not alienate, people.

In the class, the trainee should develop a tolerance for conflicts. They should become aware of their own emotional reactions to strong feelings and dogmatic statements. Furthermore, the differences between a constructive and a

66

destructive conflict needs to be discussed and illustrated. The instructor should introduce conflict or utilize strife present within the class to help sensitize trainees to the dynamics of conflict.

In the beginning class, trainees should develop skills to recognize and deal with conflict. People experience a variety of conflicts in life. They may be internal and center around the person's struggle with himself or external and involve the person's relationship with one or more people. They may be also between a person and a collective entity such as a school or church.

Conflicts may be conscious or unconscious. Often the person may experience turmoil or a sense of unrest and may not recognize that a state of conflict exists. The trainer will have a variety of conflicts to delineate and illustrate for the class.

Early man dealt with conflict in one of two ways: fight or flight. Fortunately, now conflicts may be resolved by identifying the problem, listening to complaints, seeking alternatives, gathering information, planning action, and then reviewing the outcome.

Intervening in a crisis. A crisis may be defined as a psychological state in which a person's normal coping or adaptive mechanisms no longer function. During a crisis a person becomes very vulnerable because his or her basic human balance is disturbed. Because peer counselors are often called when a crisis arises, training them to meet these challenges is very important.

A crisis affects the physical body as well as the emotional being. This effect may occur in one or several areas of the body. It may be manifested in the form of sweaty hands, a racing heart, feelings of faintness, a change of body temperature, shock, or vomiting. Prolonged physiological responses may include chronic fatigue, allergies, sleeping disorders, migraine headaches, gastrointestinal disorders, or heart problems.

A peer counselor should follow the following steps when intervening in a crisis:

1. Provide the most appropriate level of protection, security, and nurture, according to the person's obvious physical and mental needs. Activating help for survival and personal care is an important first step in a crisis.

2. Evaluate the current situation in order to identify the precipitating event. Discover what has happened in the person's life that has triggered the current stressful situation.

3. Explore why the person cannot handle the current situation as he has done with other problems in the past.

4. Define the problem in such a way that the counselee will understand and identify with it.

5. Explore alternative ways of coping with the problem and less threatening ways of viewing the situation.

6. Lend appropriate support to the counselee's efforts at managing or resolving the problem.

7. Assist in the full recovery process toward a restored balance and/or an improved level of functioning.

In the early 1940s, the crisis-intervention theory was developed by Erich Lindermann and Gerald Caplan. Crisis theory has found that equilibrium achieved by a person in crisis is dependent upon the immediacy of treatment as well as the ability and effectiveness of the person who is intervening. Therefore, it emphasizes the importance of the peer counselor's dealing with the immediate situation without probing into the counselee's chronic problems.

John Stratton states, "Examining the wide range of results that may occur from the equally wide range of methods for resolving crisis, the entire process can be seen in the two characters which make up the Chinese symbols for crisis: danger and opportunity. There is danger of a less healthy psychological and social adjustment, and there is the opportunity for growth in effectively handling a very disruptive life experience."

Peer counselors do not solve a crisis in another person's life; only the counselee can do that. However, the counselor is a guide or facilitator to the natural self-help potential of the person in crisis. The counselee may see later that the crisis was an opportunity for growth. People who have grown through a crisis often talk about the fact that they discovered new resources and skills they had never known before. For example, an unemployed person may acknowledge that getting fired from one job ultimately propelled him into a more suitable job or career path.

Crises may even bring families closer together. By experiencing the depths of a tragic loss, the family members may realize how much they mean to each other. Growth often takes place when they learn to express their caring more openly to one another. The feelings of isolation that are common to people in crisis can lead to a renewed emphasis on friendship, interpersonal networking, and community help. According to a pamphlet by Karl Slaikeu and Steve Lawhead, "New dreams, new plans, new attitudes about life can open up to people who have successfully resolved serious crises. Many find new meaning in previously dormant religious beliefs, developing more mature understandings of God."

LEARNING RESOURCES

Below is a list of training resources for the beginning class. These and others are listed in the bibliography with complete references.

Secular Resources

Robert R. Carkhuff, *The Art of Helping VI* (1987).

———, *Helping and Human Relations: A Primer for Lay and Professional Helpers,* 2 vols. (1983).

—— et al., *The Art of Helping Video Series* (1986).

—— and W. A. Anthony, *The Skills of Helping* (1979).

Gerald Egan, *The Skilled Helper*, 3d. ed. (1986).

Eugene Kennedy, *Crisis Counseling: The Essential Guide for Nonprofessional Counselors* (1981).

Dale Larson, ed., *Teaching Psychological Skills: Models for Giving Psychology Away* (1984).

Robert D. Myrick and Don L. Sorenson, *Peer Helping: A Practical Guide* (1988).

Christian Resources

Carol Lesser Baldwin, *Friendship Counseling: Biblical Foundations for Helping Others* (1988).

Gary R. Collins, *Can You Trust Psychology? Exposing the Facts and the Fictions* (1988).

——, *People Helper Pak* (1976).

Lawrence J. Crabb, Jr., *Counseling by Encouragement* (1981).

—— and Dan B. Allender, *Encouragement: The Key to Caring* (1984).

Kenneth C. Haugk, *Christian Caregiving: A Way of Life* (1984).

—— and William J. McKay, *Christian Caregiving: A Way of Life, Leader's Guide* (1986).

James H. Hightower, Jr., ed., *Caring for Folks from Birth to Death* (1985).

Stanley E. Lindquist, *Reach Out . . . Become an Encourager* (1983).

Cecil Osborn, *The Art of Understanding Yourself* (1967).

Kay Marshall Strom, *Helping Women in Crisis: A Handbook for People Helpers* (1986).

Judson J. Swihart and Gerald C. Richardson, *Counseling in Times of Crisis* (1987).

William Van Ornum and John B. Mordock, *Crisis Counseling with Children and Adolescents: A Guide for Nonprofessional Counselors* (1983).

Barbara B. Varenhorst, with Lee Sparks, *Training Teenagers for Peer Ministry* (1988).

Everett L. Worthington, Jr., *When Someone Asks for Help: A Practical Guide for Counseling* (1982).

H. Norman Wright, *Training Christians to Counsel* (1977).

6

Advanced Peer
Counseling Training

After the initial training is completed, the beginning peer counselors will be certified and ready to undertake their work. However, their training will need to continue. The peer counselors will be confronted with tough issues, and specialized training is essential in many common problem areas. This chapter presents information essential to dealing with problems related to domestic violence, drug and alcohol abuse, suicide, and death and dying.

DOMESTIC VIOLENCE

Sociologists have described America as a violent society. In the 1980s, the reported incidences of abuse and violence in the home have been dramatically increasing and are epidemic in proportion. Tragic stories of domestic violence are daily occurrences in the mass media. Most social researchers conclude that the reported incidences are only "the tip of the iceberg," with as many victims suffering in a conspiracy of silence as those who become statistics on the public record.

Domestic violence occurs between the abuser and the abused when violence becomes a part of the pattern of communication, the expression of frustration, and the method for resolving conflicts. It is indicative of a disturbed social system of rules, routines, and roles in a family that allows punishment, revenge, or hate to be expressed against one of its members, often with conscious knowledge of other members. The violence frequently results from a family history of socialization and training that leads to an intergenerational cycle of abuse. Now that more laws protect the rights of family members, domestic violence is a criminal violation that may range from assault, battery, mental cruelty, emotional abuse, child abuse, endangerment, spousal rape, physical neglect, sexual abuse, to murder.

The victims of family abuse fall into four general categories: child, sibling, spouse, and elder. Child abuse is probably the most common form of abuse and certainly has the most public awareness. Every state now has laws protecting children, and suspected abuse, by law, must be reported by agencies and professional practitioners working with children. Spouse abuse is mostly reported as battering, and the majority of victims are women. Most states have laws with criminal sanctions against marital rape or a marital partner's involuntary participation in sexual acts. Elder abuse is almost as frequent as child abuse and likely to become the major category of domestic violence given the growing number of people in the population over sixty-five years of age. Adult protective laws generally classify elder abuse as physical, psychological, emotional, and medical. Sibling abuse has to be severe and chronic before it is reported to public authorities. Intervention in situations of abuse usually occurs without serious consequences because of the difficulty in identifying a perpetrator.

The peer counselor will undoubtedly be challenged by the opportunities to help victims of domestic violence. Due to the complicated health care, legal regulations, and psychological conditions associated with domestic violence, the peer counselor's primary role is one of detection and supportive referral to more appropriate resources. The peer counselor's training in dealing with domestic violence should include the following areas: (1) learning to identify people at risk for abuse, (2) recognizing and understanding dysfunctional family systems and family life, (3) becoming familiar with the assessment profiles of the abuser and victim, (4) using crisis counseling skills, and (5) knowing basic family law, reporting responsibilities, and public agency services for domestic violence.

With supervision from a helping professional, the peer counselor may augment or provide auxiliary help to the abuser or victim being served by a primary domestic violence resource. Examples of such help include the teaching of appropriate child disciplinary procedures, the promotion of responsible self-care, the instruction of assertiveness skills, the modeling of constructive uses of personal anger, and the provision for practical assistance such as the transportation of a counselee to a self-help group for substance abusers.

DRUG AND ALCOHOL ABUSE

In the United States, the rise in drug and alcohol abuse is alarming. It has presented problems to the young and the old, the rich and the poor, the educated and the uneducated alike. Experts in the drug field tell us that every year 200,000 people are treated in hospitals for drug-related accidents and mental and physical illnesses, at least 25,000 die every year, and more than 500,000 people are arrested each year for drug-related offenses. Approximately 18 percent of the work force is operating at three-fourths capacity because of drug and alcohol abuse. Absenteeism, accidents, personnel turnover, and insurance costs push up the price of everything the public buys. To make matters worse, most drug abusers take even more drugs as a "solution" to their problems instead of trying to work them out with other people.

The peer counselor has probably known people personally who have abused drugs. Since so much has been written in books and magazines and so many television programs have been broadcast on the subject, most people already have some knowledge about drug-abuse problems. The peer counselor, however, may not have had a previous opportunity to help someone with a drug problem. During the advanced class, he or she will have the opportunity to express feelings about abusers, ask questions, and practice how to help a person through role playing.

The knowledge of five commonly abused drugs is basic to peer counseling training.

1. *Stimulants or "uppers."* They include amphetamines and cocaine. While these drugs initially produce feelings of well-being, alertness, and self-confidence, the later effect is depression.

2. *Depressants or "downers."* While stimulants speed up the central nervous system, depressants slow it down. They include such drugs as barbiturates, tranquilizers, and methaqualone. Alcohol is another common depressant.

3. *Hallucinogens.* These drugs cause changes in perception and consciousness. The common names for these drugs include "LSD," "Acid," "PCP," and "Angel Dust."

4. *Narcotics.* These drugs are derived from the opium poppy or produced synthetically. They lower the perception of pain. Included in this group are heroin, morphine, opium, codeine, meperidine, and methadone.

5. *Cannabis.* These drugs alter mood, thinking, and behavior. Included in this group are marijuana, hashish, and hashish oil.

The peer counselors will not be trained as drug counselors. Again, they will often be used as a "bridge" to get the abuser to a professional. The leader will probably want to invite a counselor from a drug-abuse-prevention agency to talk to the class. A list of agencies in the community should be made available to the peer counselors for referral use. This list may include the Drug Abuse Council, Al-Anon, Alateen, and rehabilitation centers.

While the peer counselor will be available for support and assistance, he or she must remember that drug problems can be complicated. Often the most helpful contribution they can make is to refer the person with a drug problem to a professional. Drug abusers often show slow progress, and peer counselors should expect probable discouragement.

SUICIDE

The peer counselor should be able to recognize the signs and symptoms of the potentially suicidal person. While in most cases, he or she will want to refer the counselee on to a professional, the initial contact and continuing support may be in the hands of the peer counselor.

A potentially suicidal person may tell a peer counselor about his or her plans when they would not talk to a family member. They may not want to worry the family, or they may fear that the family member will try to talk them out of it.

The counselee may not talk about suicide and actually may be seeing the peer counselor for another reason. Many suicides have been averted by an alert person listening with a "third ear" to what is being said. Most people who commit suicide give clues about what they are thinking of doing.

The peer counselor should be alert to the following signs:

- If the person has attempted suicide before, he or she may be at a high risk to try again. Individuals may casually mention the times that they have attempted suicide in the past without saying that they are considering it at the present time.

- If the person has been depressed previously and all of a sudden seems to be happy and appears to have had a burden lifted, the peer counselor should probe into what has happened. Sudden shifts in mood may mean that he or she is relieved by having decided on a plan of suicide. He or she may be happy in the belief that the pain of living will soon end.

- If the counselee appears to be extremely depressed or has had changes in personality or behavior, the peer counselor will want to look further. These changes may include weight loss, an inability to sleep, or a tendency to withdraw. Loneliness is a major factor in suicide, especially in the elderly, and the person may need to get into the mainstream of life again.

- If the counselee is threatening to commit suicide, the peer counselor must always take such threats seriously. Experts in the field of suicide estimate that threats are followed by suicide attempts at least 70 percent of the time. Instead of using the words "suicide" or "dying," the potential victim may say such things as, "I'm going away on a long trip," or, "I'm going to be moving on."

- If the counselee is making preparations for death, this signal should alert the peer counselor to possible danger ahead. The counselee may talk about getting his or her personal affairs in order, making out a will, or giving personal, treasured possessions away.

While most suicides and suicide attempts are reactions to intense feelings of helplessness, loneliness, worthlessness, and depression, one person who is available to listen can make a difference in another person's life. People who are threatening suicide are often trying to communicate their feelings of despair and are asking for help. They may feel that no solution to their problem is available or that the solutions they have attempted did not work. Looking for and finding other alternatives may make the difference between life and death to these people. The peer counselor can be instrumental in helping the counselee to see that other alternatives are available.

A peer counselor can help the counselee contemplating suicide in several ways:

1. By being alert to what the real problem is and listening for what the counselee is not saying as well as what is being said.

2. By asking the person if he or she is thinking about suicide, if the signs are apparent. Mentioning suicide does not give the counselee the idea. A suicidal person already has the idea, and talking about it openly may help to prevent the counselee from acting out the idea.

3. By indicating to the person that what is being said is being taken seriously.

4. By listening to the counselee without trying to argue or reasoning with lines like, "You can't kill yourself because your mother depends on you for support."

5. By helping the person to see that other options are available.

6. By encouraging positive action such as helping with a plan to change an existing situation.

7. By being available for the person until the crisis is over or until other help is in place.

8. By referring the counselee to a professional or a suicide-prevention service. Many people have had extensive training in suicide prevention and are more expert in the field. Instead of feeling inadequate and unsuccessful in not being able to help the suicidal person, the peer counselor should feel a great deal of

accomplishment in being able to get the counselee to a special caring resource.

DEATH AND DYING

Because death touches every family at one time or another, peer counselors will be called upon to listen to the dying person or to the grieving family or friends. Preparation for this eventuality, in the form of class discussions and role-playing exercises, will help prepare the peer counselor for this important task.

When a counselee has been told that he or she has a terminal illness, he or she may feel many unexpressed fears. Often the person does not want to talk to a family member, feeling that doing so would place an added burden on the loved one. A peer counselor is often a welcome friend.

Fears the dying person may be having include the following:

- *The fear of the unknown.* While Christians have the assurance that when their earthly lives end their spiritual life continues, some people who seek out peer counselors may not have a personal faith. Instead of "preaching" to them on their first visit, the peer counselor should listen and give them the opportunity to express this fear.

- *The fear of losing the opportunities and goals of a life.* Many people find their lives interrupted by death in middle age, or earlier, and dealing with unfulfilled dreams is often very difficult. This fear may be put into perspective by emphasizing the value of a life well lived, day by day. Furthermore, the counselor can help the fearful person pass on his or her unfinished goals to family members or a friend.

- *The fear of losing possessions.* Collectors of art or other valuable objects are often worried about what will happen to their possessions when they die. Allowing the person to talk about what options are available in planning for their disposal may alleviate some of these fears.

- *The fear of leaving behind a dependent.* Parents who provide the main source of income may experience this fear the most. However, parents of small children also face it. Again, options need to be looked at and discussed. A peer counselor is often a more likely person to fill this need, since the family members are the ones who will be the subjects of the discussion. Among other things, the dying person should be made aware of the prospect of support from other family members or close friends as well as social programs for dependents.

- *The fear of punishment.* The counselees may be concerned about how they have lived their lives. Some may be worried about fulfilling promises they have made to God in hours of need. This person needs to have past promises and opportunities clarified in a realistic manner. Where there, indeed, are shortcomings, the dying person should be encouraged to seek God's forgiveness and be appropriately assured of God's mercy.

- *The fear of not being missed or needed.* A company president may have worked all his life as if he were indispensable and may realize now that that is not the case. The counselor may remind the person of the natural and common desire to live forever. Whereas one may view his or her death as untimely, the dying person should be helped to understand the certainty of death and that this matter is usually beyond one's control. By estate planning and other methods of providing a legacy, this person can make provisions for being remembered.

- *The fear of pain.* The counselee may be wondering how much pain will come before death. His or her own ability to withstand pain may be a concern also. Along with the pain relievers provided by the medical professions, the counselor's sense of presence and expressions of love and touch are often the best resources to provide comfort for this fear.

- *The fear of being a burden.* When an illness persists, counselees may recognize that they cannot take care of their personal or financial needs. The fear of being a burden to someone else may be larger than the fear of dying. The counselor must allow the counselee the maximum degree of self-help as well as support the dependency needs of the dying person. Often it helps the person to share with loved ones the frustrations and feelings of inadequacies that are a part of the process of death.

- *The fear of loss of dignity.* Certain illnesses carry with them devastating disfigurements and limitations. A counselee may be more concerned about these conditions than is apparent to others. The counselor will need to work through whatever feelings of shame, belittlement, and depression that the counselee associates with diminished self-esteem.

- *The fear of being left alone.* The dying person may wonder if he or she will be deserted by family and friends before the end arrives. If the person has a disease that other people are concerned about contracting, he or she may have fears of rejection by society in general. The counselor can assure the person that God will always be with him or her, even in the absence of others.

In her book on *Death and Dying,* Elizabeth Kübler-Ross talks about the five stages that a dying person may go through before the end of life. The peer counselor should know these stages:

Denial. The person may refuse to believe the news that the doctor has given. Some people stay in this stage longer than others, but it is usually a temporary stage; however, denial may surface again at any time.

Anger. A counselee may question why this has happened. Finding no logical explanation, he or she may lash out in anger at the seeming unfairness of it all. The counselee may also feel guilty for feeling angry.

Bargaining. This is usually an attempt to postpone death. The peer counselor may not be made aware of this stage, since the dying person often does not tell anyone. Bargaining is usually done in secret, often with God.

Depression. When the dying person faces the fact that death is a reality, depression often sets in. It may come when symptoms of terminal illness become impossible to ignore. The counselee may express to the peer counselor his or her feelings of grief over the things already lost and the other losses which are still to occur.

Acceptance. When the dying person works through the feelings and conflicts that have arisen, he or she may now be ready to accept the fact that death will soon come. The peer counselor will recognize this as being a time of emotional calm. The counselee will have reached a state of peace.

What the peer counselor can do for the dying counselee:

1. Spend time with the person. Because this may take more time than is normally spent with each counselee, the peer counselor may want to limit the number in his or her caseload.

2. Listen patiently. The counselee may want to talk through many different issues.

3. Avoid reacting negatively to the counselee during the anger stage. Some days the counselee may appear to be angry and may direct that feeling toward the peer counselor. By realizing anger is a normal feeling for a dying person, the peer counselor will not take the words personally.

4. Explore options with the counselee. Sometimes the person may feel there are no options available in the months ahead. When he or she realizes options do exist in the life that is left, the acceptance of death will be easier.

5. Let the counselee know the peer counselor cares. Having the knowledge that someone cares and is there for them will make a difference to most people.

6. Be prepared to give spiritual guidance to the dying person. There may be occasion to help the counselee gain peace of mind by having an opportunity for a personal confession of sins. In some other cases, the counselee can be encouraged to extend forgiveness to others for their wrongdoing. To those who do not know Jesus as personal Savior and Lord, the counselor can bring the good news of salvation. The dying person can be referred to the words of the risen Lord: "I am the resurrection and the life: he that believeth in me, though he were dead, yet shall he live: And whosoever liveth and believeth in me shall never die" (John 11:25–26).

OTHER ADVANCED TRAINING SUBJECTS

With the creative use of resource materials (pamphlets, articles, books, audio cassettes, films, videotapes) and resource people (clergymen, social workers, physicians, lawyers, psychologists, former clients, etc.), the program can feature reliable and practical training throughout the year. The sequence of topics and scheduling of classes can be organized to be part of a larger lay institute or training academy operated by the church, parachurch organization, or counseling center. The classes could then serve as workshops or seminars for the general public as well as for advanced peer counselors.

Below is a list of subject areas and possible topics that a Christian peer counseling program may want to offer as part of advanced classes.

human development in the life cycle

emotions: fear, anger, guilt, and depression

values and lifestyle choices

wellness and personal health

self-improvement and individual maturity

integration of Christian faith and the behavioral sciences

role of prayer and the Bible in helping others

stress management

human sexuality and sexual problems

personal and family finances

understanding mental illness

parenting and parental guidance

helping troubled marriages

counseling with children

counseling with teenagers

counseling with single persons

counseling with remarried couples and families

counseling with older adults

ethnics and cross-cultural helping

self-help groups and organizations

professional counseling and psychotherapies
benefiting from a peer-support group

LEARNING RESOURCES

Below is a list of training resources for the advanced classes.
These are included in the bibliography with complete references.

William Backus, *Telling the Truth to Troubled People: A Manual for Christian Counselors* (1985).

David G. Benner, ed., *Baker Encyclopedia of Psychology* (1985).

John A. Bernbaum and Simon M. Steer, *Why Work? Careers and Employment in Biblical Perspective* (1986).

Billy Graham Evangelistic Association's Spiritual Counseling Department, *Christian Worker's Handbook* (1981).

Andre Bustanoby, *Being a Single Parent* (1985).

Howard Clinebell, *Basic Types of Pastoral Care and Counseling* (1984).

Gary R. Collins, *Christian Counseling: A Comprehensive Guide*, rev. ed. (1988).

————, *Helping People Grow: Practical Approaches to Christian Counseling* (1980).

Lawrence J. Crabb, Jr., *Effective Biblical Counseling: A Model for Helping Caring Christians Become Capable Counselors* (1977).

Howard L. Dayton, Jr., *Your Money: Frustration or Freedom? The Biblical Guide to Earning, Saving, Spending, Investing, Giving* (1986).

James Dobson, *Love Must Be Tough: New Hope for Families in Crisis* (1983).

Otto Ehrenberg and Miriam Ehrenberg, *The Psychotherapy Maze: A Consumer's Guide to Getting In and Out of Therapy*, rev. and updated (1986).

John Friel and Linda Friel, *Adult Children: The Secrets of Dysfunctional Families* (1988).

Gary Friesen, *Decision-Making and the Will of God* (1980).

H. D. Gray and J. Tindall, *Peer Counseling: In-depth Look at Training Peer Helpers* (1985).

Archibald D. Hart, *Feeling Free* (1979).

Grant L. Martin, *Counseling for Family Violence and Abuse* (1987).

G. Keith Olson, *Counseling Teenagers: The Complete Christian Guide to Understanding and Helping Adolescents* (1984).

Richard P. Olson and Carole Della Pia-Terry, *Help for Remarried Couples and Families* (1984).

Clifford Penner and Joyce Penner, *A Gift for All Ages: A Family Handbook on Sexuality* (1985).

Larry A. Platt and Roger G. Branch, *Resources for Ministry in Death and Dying* (1988).

Virginia Satir, *Peoplemaking* (1972).

Charles E. Schaefer and Howard L. Millman, *How to Help Children with Common Problems* (1983).

Stephen Van Cleave, Walter Bryd, and Kathy Revell, *Counseling for Substance Abuse and Addiction* (1987).

Paul R. Welter, *Family Problems and Predicaments: How to Respond* (1977).

John White, *A Christian Physician Looks at Depression and Suicide* (1982).

J. C. Wynn, *The Family Therapist: What Pastors and Counselors Are Learning from Family Therapists* (1987).

Part 3

Ministering to Others

7

True Stories from Peer Counseling in the Field of Ministry

The eight stories on the following pages are all true. Only the names and the settings have been changed to protect confidentiality. These stories illustrate how peer counseling succeeds when all the elements mentioned in the previous chapters have been put into play. The actual working together of the peer counselor and the counselee represents the finished product of the program—the counselee's receiving help. How can one better understand what peer counseling is than by seeing it in action from the viewpoint of the counselee or the counselor, as told in the stories! The authors' purpose for including the stories, therefore, is to present a clear picture of peer counseling. There are three main reasons why this is important: First, so that churches and organizations will see the benefits of the program and establish programs of their own; second, so that people having similar problems will realize that they are not alone and, like the peers in the stories, will reach out for help; third, so that peer counseling trainees will be able to read the stories and learn from them.

The peer counselors and the counselees who have shared portions of their lives have given permission for these experiences to be printed in this book. It is their hope that others will be helped, peer counseling will be spread to other churches and organizations, and Christ will be glorified.

As you read these stories, may you gain much from the experience. At the conclusion of the series, you will know more about the following: peer counseling programs and how they work on a day-to-day basis; peer counselors and the dedication and love they show to their counselees; the feelings of some Christians as they live their daily lives and sometimes find themselves in serious situations; your personal relationship to this ministry and whether you can see yourself involved in it; the way God uses people in programs that may seem new to some churches and organizations.

The stories in this chapter illustrate problems common to many people in today's society. These include divorce, remarriage, abuse, alcoholism, suicide, break down in communication between parent and child, and death and dying. The facts and details of these stories may seem hard to accept and unreal to some people; however, the ministry of a peer counselor takes him or her into the private pain and personal trauma experienced by many hurting Christians who, on the surface, may appear to be exempt from such tragedies. Many other stories could have been told, with each having its own uniqueness, but the ones chosen here were used because they represented a cross section of people of different ages, sexes, socioeconomic backgrounds, denominational preferences, and situations.

Not only are the life events in the stories true, but the peer counseling programs behind them are also real. These programs, using Christian peer counselors, are at work daily helping people in the community. Dramas, similar to those told in this book, are being revealed every day of the week to peer counselors working in Christian peer counseling programs.

The peer counseling trainees who use these stories to enhance their own skill development and understanding will want to look for the following: the interactions of the peer counselor and the counselee, including the initial contact; the decision-making process used in allowing the counselee to solve his or her own problems; the role of the peer counselor in the situation; the outcomes of the counseling sessions; and the follow-up. You may also want to consider how differently you might handle the situation if you were the peer counselor.

STEWART: A WILLING PARTICIPANT

"Thank you for your quick response on these contracts, Stewart. You really got me out of a bind. Now how about my buying you dinner tonight?" asked Victor Comb as he placed the documents just handed to him into his briefcase.

Rising from the highback chair behind his carved, walnut-grained executive desk, Stewart shook his head as he offered his hand to say goodbye. "I'm sorry, Victor, I'll have to take a raincheck on that offer, but thank you anyway. Glad to be able to look over those contracts for you. Call me if you have any other questions," the early middle-aged attorney said.

"Well it's after five o'clock already, and if you're tied up for dinner, could I at least buy you a drink on the way out?"

"I could use a cup of coffee since I won't have time to eat until after my last counseling session tonight."

"Are you seeing a psychologist?" the young real estate broker asked impulsively. After realizing what he had just said, he quickly followed up with, "I'm sorry. That's certainly none of my business. Forget I said that."

With a smile on his face, Stewart replied, "No, I'm not seeing anyone. I'm the one doing the seeing." Observing the puzzled look on Victor's face, he continued, "Come on, I'll tell you about it in the restaurant."

91

"You are a peer counselor? What ever is that?" Victor asked as the waitress placed their order on the table.

"I've been trained through a program in my church to listen to people's problems and to try to help them come up with their own solutions," Stewart said as he began the explanation of his volunteer job.

After listening intently to the full explanation, Victor repeated, almost in disbelief, the last statement he had just heard, "You do this peer counseling for three hours every Wednesday night? You can't mean for all year long? That would add up to a lot of hours, donated freely."

Somewhat amused by his colleague's look of amazement, Stewart continued, "I've done this, plus two hours of supervisory training, every week for the past seven years."

"Seven years! I can't believe it. Do you realize how much money you could have earned if you'd used those hours to see your law practice clients?"

"Man must live by more than bread alone," Stewart joked. Continuing on a more serious note, he said, "This is something very important to me, and I feel the things I have gained have more than compensated for my time."

"Such as?" Victor asked doubtfully.

"I've learned to understand myself and other people much better. I have a much broader view of the world than I did when I first began the counseling."

"How did you first begin?" Victor asked.

"In the mid-seventies, I was working with a small group, including our pastor, who was looking into the possibilities of adding this type of ministry to our church program. At the same time, I was serving as an elder in the church. So administratively, I kind of helped to get the peer counseling program going. I wasn't involved in it as a participant, but I was intrigued by it and did all I could to enable it's success."

"When did you become personally involved in it as a counselor?"

"In 1982, the director of the program came to me and

asked if I'd like to be trained as a peer counselor. I had always been more of an 'idea' person, perhaps more rational and less feeling, and helping someone else by counseling seemed a little threatening to me. However, as I thought it over I realized that this would be a good area for growth for me personally, and after all, I did believe in the program."

"I would think deciding to be a counselor would be a big step to take." Victor said.

"It was. And my main concern was I just wanted to help —and not hurt anyone. In fact, I remember saying to the director, 'The minute you think I'm not being helpful to someone, let me know, and I'll be out of the program.'"

"But you have been helpful."

"I believe so, and I, too, have benefitted. Personally I've grown out of the experience. I view the world differently than I did seven years ago. A lot of it has come from the insights I've gained in the training and the experiences I've had in dealing with people in real life situations. I have really developed a tremendous respect for people out of this whole process. We see what I would loosely call normal people with problems. They are essentially stuck, confused, or trapped, either emotionally or developmentally. And the process we often engage in involves helping them to get unstuck. We are not professionals. We don't deal with abnormal, psychological situations. We refer those out. But I've been deeply impressed with the ability of people to straighten out their lives. That is probably one of the most wonderful things I've gotten out of the program. I value peer counseling, and I've never lost my sense of amazement at being invited into another person's life. It causes a real humbleness in me."

"There must be real value in what you do."

"Yes, there is. And I think the biggest value I get out of this is having the satisfaction that I've helped a person. But you must understand, I don't solve the problem. What I try to do is to create an environment where the people can solve their own problems. And it works."

"Do they always solve their problems?" Victor asked.

"I would say certainly more than half do. But not always as expected or in the time frame originally planned. It often takes longer for a person to work through the problem than was anticipated when we began. Invariably the issue which is first presented is not the real one. They have to unlock all the boxes they are in, and this process takes time. Some people do not solve their problem because they quit working at it. They may not be hurting enough, or they just may not be motivated. There is a clear point when they stop working, and it may occur before they have solved their problem. But when they are ready to pick it up again they will be back, and I have seen this happen a number of times."

"What is the average time you see a counselee?"

"That is a good question. I'd say that it is between six months and a year. The peer counseling program was initially set up on the premise that the average time would be ten weeks, but in my experience that has not been enough time. We have a ten week review period, but we may go on if we feel more time is needed. What has actually happened is that we have adapted the policy of the program to the reality of the situation. I know the other counselors do the same thing."

"I am still amazed at all you do. Seven years is such a long time. Have you ever experienced burn-out?"

"Not really. There is probably a reason for it though. I have adhered pretty closely to a one night a week policy. Some peer counselors do two nights, but what I have committed to is what I can live with. In order to meet my family and work responsibilities, one night is all I can give."

"I can more than understand that," Victor said. Hesitating only briefly, he then said, "I guess I'm still having a hard time picturing you as a shrink. You appear so normal. Don't most of those guys have problems of their own, and that's why they become psychiatrists?"

"Please don't confuse what I do. I'm not a psychiatrist or psychologist, nor do any of the peer counselors pretend to be.

94

We are lay people who have been trained to listen to people who have everyday living problems. But to answer your question, I presume some psychiatrists do get into the profession because they started out working on their own problems, but I'm sure many do not. It's the same way with peer counseling. Some peer counselors have had problems in the past, but many have not. Personally, I've never been in therapy. I had a normal childhood, a stable home with two loving parents, and my life has been good. I'm now blessed with a loving wife and a family of my own. So you are right, I guess I'm a pretty normal guy."

"Speaking of your wife, what does she think of your spending so much time with this project?"

"She is very supportive. In fact, I'm probably a better husband as a result of being trained as a peer counselor. I know I'm a better listener."

"But doesn't your wife ever worry about some of the women becoming attracted to you? You know, in the same way women fall in love with their doctors."

"My wife doesn't need to worry, and she knows it. But, yes, on occasion a counselee will think he or she is in love with the peer counselor. That is known as transference, and we are trained to handle it."

"You mean that it has actually happened to you?"

"Yes, in all honesty it has happened. It scared me. When I figured out what was going on, I ran, not walked, to my supervisor. And one of the keys to the success in our program is the quality of supervisors we have. It is so important in situations like this. We talked it through and agreed on a plan of action which included my putting the issue on the table with her. I did this, it freed her when she realized it wasn't going any further, and then we were able to continue working on her problems."

"What did your wife think of all of this?"

"I didn't tell my wife. I explained when I first became a counselor that I would not be able to tell her about the counseling sessions. Of course, they must remain completely confidential. She understands this is a part of my life that doesn't include her, and she knows why that must be—and it's OK with her. She is really a terrific person."

"Sounds like it," Victor said with a smile. "You are fortunate to have supervisors to talk to, particularly since you can't talk it over with your wife. Do the supervisors train you in any particular theory of psychology?"

"No, our training is rather eclectic. We don't espouse a school of thought. We are not psychodynamic. We aren't behaviorist or any other particular type. But we have different teaching supervisors each year, and they clearly bring their own perspectives. So over a period of time we will be exposed to everything, and I think this is good."

"I can see now how important this is to you," Victor said. "Do you plan to do this indefinitely?"

Thinking for a moment, Stewart answered, "Yes, at the moment I plan to continue doing what I'm doing. My personal conviction is that peer counseling is of value, and people with some training, which certainly doesn't have to be a Ph.D. in psychology, can be helpful. I look at it as a privilege to be a part of this program." Glancing at his watch, he hurriedly continued, "I've enjoyed this, but I've got to get out of here. I'm going to be late for my first appointment. We'll have to talk again." Then with a smile, he added, "You've been a good listener. You might consider becoming a peer counselor yourself."

As they both stood up to leave, Victor shook his head and said, "No, thanks. I admire you, and I'm glad there are people out there doing what you do, but that's not for me." With a chuckle, he said, "Remember, I like to get paid for my hours."

Stewart said lightly as he was leaving, "Don't close the door completely. You never know what God might have planned for you."

BETTY: NO LONGER A VICTIM

"I am no longer a victim! I am no longer out of control!" The words were expressed emphatically by the attractive, thirty-five-year-old woman sitting in the circle. Others in the room could easily identify with what she was saying. A church support group made up of victims of abuse shared many similar feelings.

She continued, "Last week when I went to counseling, I made a big breakthrough. I walked in and said to Steve, my counselor, 'You know what! All my life, I've had what I call a victim's mentality. Granted, that's how I've been raised, and I'm sure that's how I chose my husband. But all of my life I've considered myself a victim and out of control with men. I've felt overpowered. But that is past!'"

Putting more emphasis on the words to make sure they were understood, she restated, "That is past! I am no longer out of control. I am in control! And I can say that I'm in control because I've given my life to the Lord to do with it whatever he wants to do. No one is going to have control over my life again except the Lord and me."

John, the newcomer to the group, looked puzzled as he stated, "I'm afraid I have joined late, and I don't know you very well, but your statements have touched me, and I'd really like to know more about what brought you to this point."

"It is not something that has just recently happened," Betty answered. "It has been going on for as long as I can remember. But it is just now, through the help of my counselors at the church's lay ministry program that I've been able to look at why I've felt such anger and hostility all my life."

"Maybe sharing your experience would help some of the rest of us," said Mary, another person sitting in the group.

Betty glanced around the circle and noticed several heads nod. She would gladly share her story if it would help someone else and witness to her faith in Jesus.

She continued, "About three years ago, I attended a seminar on child abuse. All of my life I've known there has been something wrong with me. Since the age of twenty I've been a Christian, and I love the Lord dearly, but I've had these strange feelings. It seems that all of my life I've tried to be a good Christian, but I've had problems of anger, hostility, and basic overall fear. No matter how many times I went to the Lord, I still had these feelings. I would become so angry that at times I'd even put my fist through the wall. I couldn't understand it."

As she hesitated for a moment of reflection, Don, one of the other members in the circle, said, "That must have been frightening for you."

"It was," Betty continued. "It was so scary that I decided to see a psychologist. In fact, both my husband and I attended counseling sessions for a few months because we were having marital problems. Unfortunately, we weren't able to work out our conflicts. Feeling that I was on the verge of a nervous breakdown, I decided to take our nine-year-old son and leave.

"It was really a terrible time in my life. So many things happened all at once. I moved in with my aunt; my job came to an end; I had to go out into the secular world to look for a job; great pressure was put on me because I had always worked in a church environment, and I had to learn to cope in a different working world. During that time I went through tremendous anxiety attacks, but the Lord carried me through all of it."

"But you said earlier that the feelings of fear were always with you," John stated.

"Yes, those fears kept coming back, over and over again. It wasn't until about ten years ago that I could understand any of it. At that time my mother told me the whole story. What a shock it was to learn that Jack, the man who had helped raise me and the one I had always thought was my father, was not my real biological father. It seems my mother had gotten pregnant when she was separated from Jack. My biological father left, and mother and I went to live with my grandparents. After a few years, my mother got back together with Jack, and, as my counselor said, the cards were stacked against me from that day."

"Jack knew, of course, that you were not his daughter," Mary said.

"Oh, yes, he certainly did, and he never accepted me. Jack, whom I will call my father because he is the only father that

I've ever known, was a very moody, unhappy man. He never hurt me physically, but emotionally, he abused me badly. I had a very emotionally disturbing childhood."

"Were there other children born into the home?" Sally, a pretty girl with bright red hair, asked.

"Yes, I have two younger sisters, Paula and Betsy."

"And how did your father relate to them?" Mary asked.

"My father always showed great favoritism to his first born, Paula. In fact, when I was growing up, I couldn't understand why he seemed to love her more than he did me. I just knew something was wrong because I was treated differently. I thought that it was my fault, that I must have done something to deserve this treatment. I thought if I tried harder, he would love me. But it never worked that way."

"I can relate to that," said John. "My father beat me, and I thought that it was my fault. As a result, I became a bad kid."

"Oh, I lashed out too," Betty continued. "All during my childhood, I was so angry and hostile. I beat up all the children in the neighborhood. But I never understood why I was so angry. It wasn't until years later when my mother told me about my father that some of the anger left, and I felt a little of the burden lifted."

"It sounds like you still carried some anger after that," Mary said.

"I did. It wasn't until I came to the church's lay counseling program two and a half years ago and started working through my problems that I found a sense of understanding and peace."

"Can you tell us a little about that?" John asked. "It sounds like something that I might be interested in."

"I'd be glad to because it has made such a difference in my life," Betty volunteered. "I was having problems with my teenage son, and I called the church and asked for an appointment. I was assigned to a male counselor, but I felt safe with him because a female trainee counselor sat in all the sessions with us. Of course, I didn't mention my real problem until much later because I wasn't ready at that point. I would like to add, I am really thankful for the fee arrangement of only a donation for counseling. If I'd been going to a therapist in regular practice, I wouldn't have been able to continue going financially—at least, not for the length of time that it took me to be ready to reveal my entire story."

"I don't understand what you meant about feeling safe because another woman counselor sat in on the session. Did you not feel safe around men?" Sally asked.

"No, I felt very uneasy around men. As a child I had been sexually abused by a man next door, and that, along with the emotional abuse from my father, gave me all kinds of relationship problems with men."

"Have you seen both of these counselors for the entire time?" John asked.

"Yes, but now I'm all right seeing the male counselor alone. I'm no longer apprehensive. In fact, I found that out one night when I went to the session and the woman counselor was out ill. Now I can talk about my abuse freely with both of the counselors."

"How is your relationship with Jack now?" Sally asked.

"That relationship has changed dramatically over the past three years. My mom left my dad, and he totally fell apart. Because of his personality traits, his morbidness and self-centeredness, all three of us girls have been through a living hell since that time. I can say all of these things now because I've worked through them, and I know I'm just saying the facts. For example, he would call us on the phone and say that he was going to kill himself right away. We'd rush over to his house and find the hose hooked up to the stove. This went on and on. He kept drinking more and more, but my sisters stuck to him very closely. Because I was the oldest, I tried to be there and be helpful. I recognize now that my dad has been an alcoholic for many years, and I know that I grew up in an alcoholic home."

For the first time during the evening, Susan, a quiet, plainly clothed young woman, spoke up, "My father was an alcoholic too, and all of us who were raised in his home have problems." She hesitated for a moment, and then a slight smile came over her face as she said, "But I'm getting help for mine."

Betty reached over and patted her hand and smiled before she continued her story, "After Dad had a very bad accident at work that affected his health, he started to go to church. But I felt things were not right. He started acting very differently toward me. He was no longer treating me as a daughter. Then one day when we went on a picnic he told me he didn't love me as a daughter, but he loved me as a woman. My whole life shattered at that moment. I was afraid to tell my sisters because I was afraid they would blame me or wouldn't believe me."

"Again you were a victim," John said.

"Yes, but this time I was able to talk to my lay counselors about the problem. Through counseling I worked out the terrible control that my father had always had over me. Then I was able to go to my dad and say firmly, 'I love you very much, but we are going to keep this on a father-daughter basis.' When I was able to do this, it opened up a whole new horizon for me. I can now be my own person."

"Do you ever see your dad now?" Sally asked.

"About three months ago, I attended my sister's wedding. I was able to sit next to my father, be myself, and look at him just as a person. He no longer had control over me. I looked at him and thanked God because this truly was an answer to prayer. I no longer had to be afraid of him. Since that time, I've seen him often, but the controls he once had over me are gone. It's like a big weight has been lifted."

She stopped for a moment, and there was complete silence in the room. A sense of relief and joy for Betty permeated the room. Each person seemed to share her victory.

"I am thankful for the progress that I've made," she continued. "But I recognize how much I must continue to depend on the Lord. The old patterns and thoughts want to creep back in at times, and even though they were painful—unforgiveness, bitterness, hate—they had become comfortable friends. Stepping out, away from the known patterns, was a risk, and at times, those bad feelings still knock at the door and want me to welcome them in again. But as each day passes and I meet them with God's word, I gain new strength. It has been through God's grace and the giving up of my will that I have been able to forgive my father. And I know that God has used the counseling program at this church as a way for me to receive His help."

John's attention had not waned for one moment all during the time Betty had been talking. When she concluded her last sentence, there was a moment of silence, and he then said, "Thank you, Betty, for sharing your story. I'm new in this support group, and I've learned a lot from you tonight." Then on a less serious note he added, "Do you ever wonder about your biological father?"

Smiling, Betty responded, "I know that it doesn't matter who my biological father is as long as I know my Heavenly Father."

JIM AND KAREN: A MARRIAGE SAVED

"It definitely saved our thirteen-year marriage," Karen spoke softly but with a conviction in her voice that wasn't to be doubted.

"I don't understand how seeing someone that you call a peer counselor could make so much difference," Sally pondered. Not waiting for an answer, she continued, "But it is obvious just from being around you and Jim today that things have changed. I can see and *hear* the difference. When Paul and I were your house guests a few years ago, the tension was so thick between the two of you that it could have been cut with a knife."

The same old Sally, thought Karen. Her irrepressible college roommate had not changed in the many years she had known her. She was still the uninhibited, lay-it-on-the-line and tell-it-as-it-is, lovable, devoted person that Karen had met her first day at college. Karen still remembered when her new redheaded, chubby roommate walked into their dorm room with suitcases in hand and before introducing herself said, "We will get along just fine as roommates as long as you don't borrow my clothes or try to steal my boyfriends."

It was easy to heed Sally's instructions because Karen's 5'8" slender frame could hardly wear the same clothes as her roommate's 5'3", somewhat overweight body. As for boyfriends, Karen never needed to take anyone's away because she always had more offers of dates than her heavy college schedule allowed her to accept.

The friendship of the roommates had been immediate and long lasting. Even though they had parted and moved to different parts of the country, they had remained in contact, making visits to see each other every few years.

Smiling, Karen responded, "Oh, you noticed, did you! Well those days are gone. So let's talk about something more pleasant."

"But I'd really like to hear about what happened to you and Jim," Sally insisted, adding in a more serious tone, "Things haven't been going exactly great with Paul and me lately. Maybe this idea of talking to a peer counselor would help us."

Seeing the pensive look on her friend's face, Karen said, "Sure, what would you like to know?"

"First, I'd like for us to finish loading the washer and then join Jim and Paul in the living room. I think it would be a good idea for both Paul and me to hear what you and Jim have to say. That is, if you don't mind talking in front of the men."

"Of course I don't mind. Communication is what this is all about."

Settling into the overstuffed chair in the small, tastefully decorated living room, Karen said to her husband, "Sally would like to hear about what we've been doing once a week for the past two years."

Looking somewhat puzzled for a moment, Jim slowly smiled and said, "Oh, you want to hear about the other woman I've been seeing every week."

"Don't let him kid you," Karen good-naturedly joked, "I was with him on every visit."

"I'm lost," Paul injected. "Did I come in on the middle of a conversation, even though I've been in the room all the time?"

"Karen and I have been seeing this wonderful lady who is a peer counselor at one of the local churches," Jim explained.

"At your church?" Paul asked.

"No, at a church which serves not only their own members but also members of other churches in the area which do not have a peer counseling program."

"Funny that you would mention peer counseling because I was reading an article in a magazine just the other day about that course being taught in a high school. But how does that fit in with you and Karen?" Paul questioned.

"Let me answer that," Karen responded. "Jim and I were having difficulties with our marriage. I had reached the point where I felt like I really needed to see someone, so I called my church, and they recommended Hillview Presbyterian Church's peer counseling program. I followed through with their suggestion and began to meet with Linda, our peer counselor, at the church every week."

"But I thought you said you and Jim saw the counselor together," Paul responded.

"That wasn't until a few months later," Karen continued. "I had been seeing a therapist during a previous point in our marriage, but I knew we could not financially afford that kind of help at the present time."

"While Karen was quite comfortable seeing a counselor, I wasn't," Jim interjected. "I'd always been against that sort of thing. We had gone to a therapist about eight years before, and I had thoroughly disliked his methods. It confirmed what I felt about counseling."

"The therapist had been helpful to me," Karen quickly

stated, "but he and Jim just did not hit it off. Because of this, I knew that Jim wouldn't go, so I just decided to go by myself. Then after a while Linda said that she really needed to see us together. She asked if it would be all right if she called Jim and invited him. I told her to go ahead but not to be disappointed if he didn't come."

"What did she say that got you there, Jim?" Sally wanted to know.

"She asked if I would come just the one time. I agreed to just one visit. But when I went to see Linda, it was different. I realized she was unbiased, fair, warm, and wanted to hear what we had to say. It ended up being an enjoyable experience, which I didn't think it would be."

"So you continued to go with Karen each week," Paul commented.

"Yes, I guess I did, but Linda didn't ask for a long-term commitment from me. She would just ask at the end of each session if I'd come back the next time." Laughing as he spoke, Jim said, "She is a pretty bright lady."

With growing interest in the conversation, Paul said, "I want to ask you what this bright lady you are describing did? But before I ask that question, I think I need a little background on why you were there in the first place. You two always seemed like you had so much going—that is, until our last visit with you about three years ago. After we left, Sally and I commented about the tension that seemed to be building up between the two of you."

"You were so right. Things were going from bad to worse. At that point there was no way to hide the tension," Karen confessed.

Jim nodded, "We were having problems before, but Karen's getting pregnant brought things to a head. We went through a real crisis at that time."

"You had been married for ten years, but you weren't ready for children yet?" Paul asked.

"I had visions of getting back into the music world, but I

knew if we had children, that dream would never be fulfilled."

"Jim, would you mind filling us in on your background? I've heard bits and pieces from Sally, but you and I have never talked about it," Paul said.

"There really isn't much to say," Jim said modestly. "My father was a concert violinist in Germany before the war. In fact, I was born there. But, during the war, my parents lost all of their land and everything they owned. As soon as the war was over, they brought me to the United States and started life all over again. Because the philharmonic orchestras did not pay well enough in those days, my father had to look for something else to do to support my mother and me. He bought a dry cleaning business, worked very hard, and made it successful."

"I didn't know you played the violin!" Sally exclaimed.

"I don't. When I talk about a musical career, I'm talking about singing and writing songs."

"Don't you remember, Sally? Jim was singing with a band when I met him."

"I know that!" Sally replied impatiently. "He did that after you were married, too."

"Up until the time my father died," Jim remarked. "Then I knew I had to go back to California and take over the family business. I remember flying back to Los Angeles, thinking my fun was over. But deep down I still thought that some day I would get the music going again. In fact, I was practicing with a group when Karen called me to tell me she was pregnant. I kind of fell apart. My vision of getting back into the music business would never come true."

"That's when you began drinking," Karen injected.

"Yes. I know. It wasn't easy on a pregnant wife."

"So, basically your problem was related to Jim's career," Paul said.

"Not just that," Karen stated. "We'd had trouble off and on, and I feel the root of it was lack of communication. Learning to communicate is something that should be required before anyone gets married."

"You don't feel that it just comes naturally?" Sally asked.

"For me it didn't," Karen said. "It's been very difficult for me to learn to communicate. It had not been there when I was growing up. I wasn't allowed to express my feelings without being put down. As a rebellious teenager, I never learned how to communicate."

"Our backgrounds were very different too," Jim stated. "Even though I grew up in the United States, I was raised as a pre-war German child. I found Karen doing things that would have been very disrespectful in my parents' home."

"Sounds like this might lead to in-law problems," Paul said.

"It wasn't just in-law problems on Jim's side. It was also on my side," Karen volunteered. "My dad and mom divorced ten or eleven years ago. Mom is happily remarried and lives in Florida, but Dad's second marriage didn't work out. He married a woman with three children, and he isn't a very patient man. His marriage lasted only seven years."

"Karen's dad is a nice man, but when he comes to visit, he wants to fix everything in the house—and I guess I resent that," Jim said haltingly.

"Wish you'd send him over to our house," Paul said. "I could keep him busy for quite a while."

"It wasn't that I didn't have things that needed doing," Jim continued. "But he would do things without even asking if I wanted them done. And often he didn't do it the way I had envisioned doing it. I know it may sound minor, but I can assure you that I began to dread his visits."

"I didn't like the way he came in and took over, either," said Karen. "But he is my dad, and it was difficult for me to say anything. I think it was his way of trying to show love. I don't think he realized what a problem he was causing. It has always been difficult for me to communicate with my dad, and often I felt caught in the middle between him and Jim."

"But it wasn't just Karen's father that caused problems,"

said Jim. "My mother lived in the same city, and dealing with her was more of a day-to-day trial."

"Such as?" questioned Sally.

"She thought our first child should be potty trained at ten months," volunteered Karen. "But I held firm on that one and did not train him until he had passed his second birthday."

"Things are better between the two of you now though," stated Jim.

"Yes. Much better. I see Jim's mother once a week now. We have lunch, and it is a very pleasant visit. I've had to put aside things that have happened in the past—so has she."

Recapping, Paul said, "You've had problems relating to an unfulfilled career, different family backgrounds, and in-laws. That's quite a bit. This peer counselor must have been good."

"Yes, she was. There was also another problem," said Karen. "I had worked for ten years. When I got pregnant, I quit work, and we had to learn to live on a single income. That was hard. Particularly when Jim's business is somewhat unpredictable, and we could not really count on a certain amount each month."

"And this peer counselor helped you with all of these problems?" Sally asked. "Just what did she do?"

Karen answered, "She helped me to get in touch with my feelings. It took some time to get through the layers of emotion and to really see why I felt the way I did. It is still a process I'm working on—and will be the rest of my life."

"Can you give us an example?" asked Paul.

"I thought I was always angry. Linda helped me put different labels on my emotions. Sometimes I was feeling fear, hurt, or frustration—but I always labeled it anger. When I learned to recognize what I was feeling, then I was able to deal with it."

Jim joined in, "She has helped me to see things that I've never been able to admit before. At one time, I felt like Karen and Linda were ganging up on me. Linda even asked if I would like to have another peer counselor, a man, meet with the three of us. I declined. I knew that Linda was fair and was just getting things out on the table. It's hard to look at your own faults, though, and admit they belong to you."

"She also helped me to realize that what I thought I was saying was not what Jim was hearing," stated Karen.

"What do you mean?" asked Paul.

"I would say something to Jim, and then Linda would ask Jim to repeat what I had said. What Jim repeated was not what I had intended to say."

"We learned to make sure we knew what the other person was saying before we became angry at what we thought we heard," Jim said.

"I've also learned to not expect Jim to automatically know how I feel. I use to get angry because I felt that he should have picked up my clues as to how I was feeling. Now I tell him. I don't leave it to chance, and I don't get my feelings hurt. It is much easier this way."

"We've also learned to use 'I' messages," Jim said. "Instead of always saying, 'You do this and you do that' and getting the defenses up, we now try to say things like, 'I feel frustrated by what is happening.' Communication is a lot easier when one person is not accusing the other person."

"Those things sound like they would be helpful for anyone to know," Sally said.

"Good communication is helpful no matter where you use it," said Karen. "But meeting with Linda involved more than just learning good communication skills. She has listened and helped us work out problems, including brainstorming alternatives which we hadn't thought of before. There is the spiritual side too. Linda is a Christian, and we have been able to look at things from a biblical perspective. Our Christian faith is very important to us, and having someone listen to us who understands our values and knows where we are coming from has been one of the most important things about our counseling experience."

"We have a lot of friends who are divorced," said Jim. "And it would have been very easy for us to have given up and gotten a divorce too. But we had Linda there to keep encouraging and working with us. She never gave up, not even at one point when both of us were very discouraged and didn't know if we could work it out."

"I feel very fortunate that we are still together," said Karen. "We seemed to know that we had something too good to give up on—we had a certain tenacity that I know we still have."

"But how could you afford two years of counseling?" Sally asked. "I know that Paul and I couldn't."

"That is one of the things that makes peer counseling so special," Karen explained. "The peer counselor is trained at church and does not charge for the sessions. The church where we met with Linda did ask for donations to help keep the program going, but no one is expected to give more than he or she can afford."

"We have referred some of our friends who are having problems," said Jim. "We would be reluctant to refer them to a therapist, knowing how difficult money is to come by for young families. But we don't hesitate to refer them to a peer counselor. We know they can afford that."

"As you have seen, we had many problems," Karen began, "and it has taken a period of time to work through them. There is no way that we could have continued to see a therapist for this long."

"And we still see Linda from time to time," Jim emphasized. "After we stopped seeing her every week, we started seeing her once every two weeks. And now it is just when we feel we need it."

"Linda has become a very dear friend," Karen said softly. "Although we don't see each other on an outside basis, she is still very special. When you allow someone to get to know you as well as Linda knows us, then that person becomes a dear friend."

"It sounds like the two of you have come a long way," Paul said.

Looking at each other, Jim and Karen smiled. "It *has* been a long way," Karen said. "We started out blaming each other for our problems, instead of working them out as two adults. I'm really convinced the Lord has helped us through all of this. Peer counseling and Linda were the tools He used."

"I wonder if there is a church with a peer counseling program in our area?" Sally asked.

"Let's look for one when we get home," Paul said.

"That's great," said Jim. "I know what a difference it can make."

Rising from his chair and winking at Karen, Jim continued in a voice filled with glee, "How would you like to hear a new song I've written? This may be the one that gets me back into the music world."

CLAUDIA: UP FROM DESPAIR

The setting was beautiful for a weekend retreat. Tall pine trees reached up toward the blue, cloudless sky. The air was clean and cool, just right for a brisk walk by the mountain stream. What a wonderful place for a peer counseling retreat, and this one was living up to all the expectations of the group.

The guest speakers during this particular weekend were outstanding, and they were being received with warmth and appreciation. Beverly Swanson, a well-known Christian author had just spoken, and she was now opening the session for group discussion and questions.

"How did you become trained as a peer counselor?" Ralph, a new counselor attending his first retreat, wanted to know.

"A peer counseling program was started at my church seven years ago, and I joined the first class. We were trained by a licensed marriage, family, and child counselor and a licensed clinical social worker. For six months we met every week for two hours. After completing this beginning class, I took an advanced class for another year."

"I know you have worked with many interesting counselees. Would you tell us your most successful experience in helping someone?" Julie, a vivacious redhead, asked.

"As you know, each peer counseling session is confidential, but I can tell you about this one because I am using it for a story I am writing for a magazine. The person, whom we will call Claudia, has given me permission to tell her story if I do not use her real name."

"Would you start from the very beginning? I am a brand new peer counselor, and I am very interested in learning all the details of helping someone," a portly man on the back row interjected.

"OK, if that's the way you want it," Beverly responded. "I was at home one day when I received a call from my pastor. He told me a woman was in his office who had come to him for help. He went on to say that he thought I should be the one to see her because he believed I could be helpful. He told me that she was talking about suicide and asked me to come right on down to his office. I hesitated for a moment because I felt the enormous responsibility of taking on a potentially suicidal counselee. My pastor re-emphasized that he really thought that I could help her, so I left what I was working on and headed for the church."

"I can imagine what you did all the way there," Julie said.

"You are right! I prayed! I knew that the Holy Spirit must guide me. But little did I know at that time the seriousness of the situation and how much I really would need to depend on God. When I got there, I found an attractive, tall, slender blonde sitting in the pastor's office crying. After we were introduced and the pastor explained that I was there to help her, he left the two of us alone. Claudia was very receptive to my being there. I remember I pulled the chair up very close to her because I felt she needed a human touch. Then I asked what was making life intolerable for her. She opened up and talked freely."

112

"You were fortunate that she was willing to express her feelings," Richard, a retiring little man, said.

"You are right, and I was praying that I would be used by God to help her—the Holy Spirit really does lead in these situations. I was with her for two hours. The first hour she just talked, and I listened. The second hour she was able to release some of her tension, and by the time she left she told me that she would not kill herself. During those two hours, she told me an incredible story. After our session, I had a lengthy telephone conversation with our program consultant. We discussed my peer counseling with a suicidal person, and he advised me to work closely with her professional therapist, with whom she still maintained contact. She had so many different problems that over the next weeks, I had to network her to many different people. I even went with her one time to a community agency for financial assistance. Also, the program consultant arranged for her to have a meeting about her finances with one of the businessmen in our church. Fortunately, there were a lot of people willing to help, and she was ready to grow."

It was Ralph again who asked, "Would you mind telling us some of her problems?"

"Her background was unbelievably abusive, from her early years and on throughout her adult life. She experienced things that most people would never imagine could take place. For example, her father got her pregnant when she was a teenager, and he had someone go to her house and do an abortion on the kitchen table. He then made her get up and go outside and bury the baby. She still shudders when she recalls that the ground was frozen, and it was very difficult to get the shovel into the earth."

"I have never heard of anything so cruel!" Julie said with a painful look on her face.

"Unfortunately, it doesn't get better for her. She married a man who became involved in cults, and he demanded inhuman things of her. Her husband was bringing men home and requiring her to sleep with them, and she was saying, 'I can't. I can't. I love God, and I can't.' This was her second marriage, and she was trying to raise and protect her three little boys by her first husband."

"She was a Christian?" asked a young lady in the second row.

"Yes, she had an older woman—a wonderful Christian lady—kind of adopt her and take her under her wing when she was a young adult. This grandmotherly soul had a profound influence on her life. She mothered her and did some beautiful reprogramming with her, but the best thing she did was to lead Claudia to Christ, and I think it is a real tribute to the grace of God and her faith in Him that she was able to pull through her tragic life and keep her sanity. She is such a strong and practical person, and I have been so blessed by getting to know her. That is one of the great things about peer counseling. God uses us to help in incredible situations. If you offer yourself, you will receive something you couldn't have in any other way."

"What is Claudia doing now?" Ralph asked.

"She ended up having to dissolve her second marriage, and she is now married to a good man who loves her dearly. She has moved out of the state, but I hear from her frequently. In fact, I have a letter with me that I received soon after she moved. I'll read you part of it."

After reaching into her purse and bringing out a well-worn piece of stationery, Beverly began to read Claudia's words, "No one in professional counseling helped me as you did because no one taught me about joy. They took me apart and spread me out like peanut butter, and, yes, I did come to understand some things about myself, but they never helped me get back together and have something to live for. Over and over you said, 'God wants you to enjoy the life He has given you. He wants to give you joy.' And that was news to me."

Beverly lay the letter on the podium and said, "I thanked God for the privilege of helping this woman. For many years, Claudia had been in therapy with a psychologist who had helped her by using hypnosis and valid counseling techniques to work through some of the incredible problems of her background. But that person wasn't a Christian, and he couldn't offer her joy through the Holy Spirit. I think the Christian peer counselor is in a very unique position to bring that to someone."

"Is Claudia having a better life now?" Julie wanted to know.

"Yes, in many ways. God has given her such a ministry to others. She has tremendous insight into human nature, partially because she has had so much therapy and has been through so much pain herself. I remember the inspirational benefit she received during our time of peer counseling from regular attendance at our worship services, which undoubtedly continue to provide strength for her. I wish that all of you could have the opportunity to get to know this woman. She is such a spunky person with an unusual amount of courage. One that does not run to the 'comfort zones,' but just heads right straight into the problem and works it out. She is 'street smart,' with practical forthrightness and complete honesty. But I don't want to leave the impression that lately life has been a bed of roses for her. That isn't true. Since she has moved, she has undergone two different surgeries on her back, but her faith keeps her going. As I said, I have learned so much from this woman, and I really feel blessed to have her as a friend."

"And I feel blessed because you have shared this story with us," the portly man on the back row said. "Because you have had so much experience and most of us are just beginning, I wonder if there is any other word that you'd like to leave with us?"

"I would like to encourage all of you peer counselors to be yourselves. You do not have to put on some kind of peer counseling garb. The unique thing about this ministry is that God takes your personalities and uses the strengths and sometimes the weaknesses to bring about understanding."

She paused for a brief moment and continued, "I would also like to see you spread this program. I think everyone in the church should be trained to recognize when a person has a serious problem and to get them to the help they need. This could be a valuable service for the church to provide. Too, peer counseling could be integrated into other existing programs. I do discipleship training, but first I do five weeks of peer counselor training with the class. I put it at the very beginning before we go into one-on-one discipleship training because I find when I do either peer counseling training or discipleship training, I cannot separate one from another. New Christians who are having real-life problems need to find help in working them out."

Looking over the faces in the audience and finding she still had their undivided attention, she said, "One last thought I want to leave with you. When you are counseling, you don't always see the results. With Claudia I was fortunate that I saw great growth, but this is not true of every one of my counselees. Just remember, God is able to use our most feeble efforts, even if we are not aware of the outcome."

HELEN: RECOVERING FROM AN ALCOHOLIC HOME

"I grew up in an alcoholic family. Both of my grandfathers were alcoholics, and so was my father. My father killed himself when I was twenty. Then Mother began drinking. She will not admit it, but she is an alcoholic, too." The short, crisp, to-the-point sentences were spoken by Helen, a beautiful, well-educated woman in her mid-thirties.

Rhonda looked at her fellow teacher in disbelief. "You must be kidding me," she said. "Children of alcoholics are supposed to have problems, and you are the most organized, well-prepared, dedicated teacher on this campus. I haven't known you but a few months, but it has been long enough for me to know that I'd give anything to have it 'all together' like you do."

"Thank you for the compliment, but I can assure you, I haven't always been this way. There were times during the past years when I felt that life wasn't worth living. At one point, all that mattered to me was getting my three sons raised, and after that I wouldn't need to care about life."

The janitor came into the room to remove the wastepaper baskets which were filled with scraps of paper from the day's activities of the fifth-grade class. However, the two women didn't seem to notice. Everyone else had left at the close of the day, but Rhonda had seen Helen's door open as she walked by and had stopped to say hello. Now she couldn't help but think how ironic it was that people with similar situations seemed to be drawn together.

"I'm so glad you've shared this with me," Rhonda said. "Now I know why you understand my pain so well."

"Pain is something I do understand. It has taken extreme effort on my part in seeking help and knowledge to overcome my problems. All of my life, I've carried the burden of how to repair the damages of an alcoholic family."

"How have you sought help?"

"I've attended Al-Anon meetings, Bible study weekend retreats, and for the past year, I've met each week with a peer counselor from my church."

"A peer counselor? Has that helped?" Rhonda asked.

"It has been extremely helpful in many different ways."

"Could you give me an example?"

"Of course. First of all, it gives me a real good sounding board. The peer counselor is nonjudgmental, and I know that I can be completely honest with her, and she will not think badly of me. Also, I get a lot of positive feedback from her, and I don't get that any other place in my life. Another main reason is I always feel so much better after I spend an hour in a session. It is very therapeutic for me."

"Those sound like good reasons for seeing a counselor," Rhonda stated.

"An additional reason I didn't mention it is the fact that it has always been hard for me to ask for help, but seeing my counselor is different. I don't mind asking her for help. She

117

seems to really care about me as a person, and I know she wants to see me solve my problems."

"Are your problems like mine? Are you really angry?" inquired Rhonda.

"I used to be," Helen said. "I was always a strong-willed child. I needed nurturing, but I didn't get it. I was the oldest of three children, and for some strange reason my father thought he should teach me boxing. I thought it was necessary for existence back then, and I used it to beat up all the other kids in the neighborhood. Soon I had quite a reputation in the community, and no one came near me. My perception of the world was that it was a 'slug-out contest.' At the time, I didn't realize that I was using it as a release for my anger."

"I can't help but laugh at the thought of your beating up on all those kids," Rhonda said with a chuckle. "Wouldn't the kids in your class be surprised to hear about your childhood! You are always so beautifully dressed, so poised and cultured. They wouldn't believe it."

"I can hardly believe it myself. But I can't believe other parts of my life either. Who would have thought when I was growing up in an affluent neighborhood, with a father who had a good position in the business world and who drank only when he was at home, that anything could have been wrong? I was a good kid in school—always did my homework and made good grades. I was accepted by a major university. What more could I want, most people would think. But they didn't know the problems that went on in our home when my father drank. He became a different person, a violent man. Everyone in the house was very afraid of him."

"Your life must have gotten better after he died," Rhonda concluded.

"I wish I could say that it did, but that is far from the truth. After Dad died, Mother began to drink. Two years later I was married and grateful to be away from that environment. But if I thought my life was bad then, after I got married it was worse."

"Don't tell me! I know! You did exactly what I did and married an alcoholic like your father," Rhonda said.

"Not exactly. Steve didn't drink at all before we were married, but he got into financial trouble a few years later and began to drink at that point. While my father had some positive traits, my husband had very few. He was a very possessive man."

"Then he wasn't the man you thought you had married."

"Not at all. He went through a distinct change after we got married. I will never forget the time he locked me in a room. However, I understood his actions better when I got to know his family and saw how cruelly they treated each other. After a few years, I couldn't take it any longer. I took our three children and moved in with my mother."

"That must have been difficult," Rhonda said in a whisper.

"Mother's house was small, and I slept on the couch for six years. But I was thankful for a place to stay. On my salary, I couldn't pay rent and support three young boys. Never in my wildest dreams did I ever think I'd be supporting three children by myself."

"But at least you were out of a bad marriage."

"Well, yes and no. Steve didn't want the divorce, and he fought me all the time for custody of the children. One summer, we spent ten weeks in court. I think it was more difficult being divorced from him than it was being married to him."

"But you are engaged to someone else now, and the future will be a lot brighter, won't it?" Rhonda asked.

"I hope so. I still have a lot of fears about getting married again. Life is very dangerous; the world is a dangerous place. That has been my reality, and I have to constantly tell myself that things are all right, I'm safe."

"You said counseling had helped you accept a more positive attitude."

"With counseling, it has been as if someone let me out of jail. I am no longer at the mercy of the way I was raised. Peer counseling has been helping me establish healthy relationships. I have such a good relationship with the Lord that I feel that no matter what happens I'm safe. And growing up I didn't feel safe at all."

"You have come a long way already."

"I feel so much healing from what I know I suffered as a child. I am much more capable of living with my emotions and being thankful for what I have. I need to continue to remind myself to make much less of my shortcomings. As you know, I'm a perfectionist, and I put a lot of pressure on myself to make everything come out just right."

"Your classroom is always decorated so beautifully," Rhonda observed.

"Speaking of decorating, that is something else that I talk to my counselor about, and she understands when no one else seems to care. I'm decorating my house now—what a relief to have a place of my own—and no one understands why I have to have the towels match the soap and all the other little details. But those things are important to me."

"It sounds as if you can talk to your counselor about almost anything."

"I really can. She is helping me now with some fears that have surfaced since I've been engaged."

"Fears?" Rhonda asked.

"My fears of remarriage are great. My counselor has been extremely helpful because I don't have a normal kind of balance in seeing relationships as they really are. Since I haven't experienced what one might call a normal life, my basic understanding of a male-female relationship is not a healthy one. My counselor has been helping by allowing me to talk about my fears and concerns, and I'm convinced with her and the Lord's help, I'll continue to work out these fears."

"I don't have any doubts about it. I know you will," Rhonda said as she walked toward the door. Turning and smiling as she entered the hallway, she called back over her shoulder, "Remember, tenacity is one of your strengths. Just hang in there."

Six months after that conversation, Helen was married. When she returned to school after a short trip, she confided in Rhonda once again.

"It was a real act of courage for me to go through with the wedding because I was very frightened. For several weeks before the date, I suffered from symptoms of stress. You know, the classic ones—heart palpitations, headaches, skin rash, stomachaches. I guess I truly was panic-stricken."

"But you did go through with it," Rhonda said.

"Yes, but it would have been very easy for me to have 'bailed out' because I had once before."

"You mean you had called off a wedding before this one?"

"That's right. I was engaged to a really nice man, but when it came time for the ceremony, I just couldn't go through with it."

"What gave you the courage to do it this time?" Rhonda asked.

"I prayed a lot about it, and I talked to my counselor frequently. I remember seeing her one time when I was in tears. Actually, I was a real basket case. I told her I thought I was about to make a big mistake. It was really frightening for me to think of putting so much of my life into someone else's hands. She was patient and allowed me to cry and talk through it. That seemed to be a turning point, and a week before the wedding I became calmer. In fact, on the actual day of the wedding, I felt very calm."

"And how do you feel now?" asked Rhonda.

"I know that I made the right decision. I am very happy."

"And I'm happy for you." With those words, Rhonda walked over to Helen, gave her a hug, and said with a smile, "Now do you think we could look for a husband—for me?"

ALICE AND CYNTHIA: LEARNING TO COMMUNICATE

"Short-term counseling was all we needed," said the attractive, middle-aged, professional woman. My daughter and I attended only seven sessions with the peer counselor, and by that time we accomplished our goal of opening up communication between the two of us."

"If I thought going to counseling would help me understand Tony, I would start tonight," confided her next-door neighbor. Shaking his head, the tall man with greying temples went on to say, "Ever since Edith died, Tony has been closed as tight as a jar with the lid on it. I never know what he is thinking or how he is truly feeling. His mother's death had a profound impact on him."

"Well, Ken, I can't predict if counseling would work for you and Tony, but I certainly know that it did for Cynthia and me."

"Could you tell me a little more about it, Alice?" Ken asked.

Placing her gardening tool on the ground, she walked over to the empty lawn chair beside Ken's and sat down. It had been over six months since Edith's death, and today was the first time Ken had crossed over to her yard to visit. He had been sitting and watching her dig in her flower bed for nearly half an hour. She sensed his own need for companionship. "Of course, I'll be happy to," she said. "What do you want to know?"

"How did you find this peer counseling program?"

"It is a ministry of our church. I have known other people in the church and the community who have received help, so I immediately thought of going there when Cynthia and I started to have problems. I knew enough about counseling to know the type of help we needed did not require a professional counselor. All we needed was someone to help us get through some of the communication barriers. I felt peer counseling would be perfect for our situation."

"It has been four years since you and Gary were divorced. Did the problem with Cynthia start immediately afterwards?"

"No, it only started after she moved back home with me about a year ago. You remember she lived with Gary for over a year. Then, after she graduated from high school, she moved

122

into an apartment with a girlfriend. By that time I'd been living alone in the house for two years, and I really loved it. The house was so peaceful and quiet. All the turmoil and tension which had gone on before the divorce was over with, and I was extremely happy by myself. Cynthia kept saying to me when she would visit, 'Oh, Mom, you are so lonely.' I would try to make her understand I was not lonely, and I'd say to her, 'Please don't worry about me. This is wonderful.' But I guess she didn't believe me."

"But why then did you invite her to move back home?" Ken asked.

"I didn't. She was living on her own, and I thought she was doing just fine. Every time I would see her, she would say things were wonderful, and I chose to believe her. I had designed my new life the way I wanted it. I was busy traveling with my work and enjoying my freedom. But one night she called me at 2 A.M. sobbing and crying and asking if she could move home. I told her that it was the middle of the night, and I couldn't think clearly. So I invited her to have dinner with me the following weekend. The next Friday night we had dinner, and she still wanted to come back home."

"I can imagine all the things that must have been going on in your head," Ken said with a smile on his face.

"You're right. I was apprehensive about it working out, but I set down certain rules with her. I told her she was old enough that she should pay some rent, and I explained she couldn't just come running home because it was free. I went on to say I had my own life and she had hers, and I told her I wasn't so sure that all of this was going to work out. But she had it all figured out. She was going to help me with the house, and all of a sudden she was going to be an adult. So I said, 'Fine, let's give it a try.'"

"A mother's love never stops trying," Ken said, shaking his head.

"Don't paint any halos over my head because after about six months, I was really feeling frustrated. She had moved back in and had continued acting like a teenager but wanted the freedom of an adult. She was willing to pay the minimal rent, but she didn't want to cleanup after herself or help me at all around the house. I became more and more frustrated."

"Couldn't she take care of her chores on the weekend?" asked Ken.

"On the weekend, she was always gone with her boyfriend. When I would tell her this arrangement just wasn't working, she'd refuse to talk about it, slamming the door as she left the room. This was a pattern her father had mastered when he was still in the house. He would leave when there was any kind of an argument."

"Like father, like daughter," Ken mumbled softly.

"But that wasn't all. I began to realize more and more she was doing things right under my nose she knew I wouldn't approve of. She would sometimes leave for days and wouldn't call. By this time, I was really concerned. But she continued to refuse to talk about our problems. I knew we needed to see someone who would help us break this communication barrier. There was definitely a wall built up between the two of us which I couldn't get past."

"That is when you went to the peer counseling at the church," Ken remarked.

"Yes, and we both found it very helpful. I think the best thing it did for us was make her sit in the room for the entire hour without being able to walk out the door—and we were able to talk. This was a real benefit, because she started saying things which were quite profound. I had a feeling these thoughts were inside her, but she had never been able to express them before."

"The counselor saw both of you together?"

"In the very beginning, he saw Cynthia alone, but we met together most of the time."

"Did the counselor give you good advice?"

"Giving advice is not really what peer counselors do.

They listen and try to help their counselees solve their own problems."

"How?" Ken asked.

"We started talking about the problems of two adult women living in one home which originally had been established on the basis of a mother-daughter relationship. How do you switch that relationship from mother-daughter to two adults? We talked about the need for respect, for me to stop treating her like a teenager—even though I thought she was still acting like one—and for her to treat me like an adult instead of an authoritarian mother. We also talked about the differences in our lifestyles; in her generation going off for the weekend with a boyfriend is the thing to do, but in my generation it isn't. This bothered me, but what was more distressing was the fact she would not discuss the issue with me. In the counseling session we talked about this as well as other big issues."

"Big issues?"

"Oh, yes. One time we got into a real shouting match in the counseling office over how she bought her car. We really screamed at each other, but it was good to vent all the pent up emotions. At least, I know it was for me. I was really angry."

"You were angry because she bought a car?"

"No, I was angry because she did it behind my back. While I was away on a business trip, Cynthia really got taken by the car deal she made. She bought it on the day I left and was talked into paying an extremely high interest rate for the car loan. She has enormous car payments and high insurance premiums."

"Sounds like she acted unwisely," Ken confirmed.

"The thing that really hurt me was the fact she had moved back in with me under the pretense that she wanted to save money to go back to school and to buy a car. With her modest salary and extremely high car payments, I knew that she wouldn't be able to move from the house for at least three years, and this was not our agreement when she moved home. But we talked it out, and we were able to get the anger out into the open instead of keeping it bottled up inside of us. This was a real breakthrough for us."

"Then you feel the communication barriers were broken?"

"I feel that in the sessions we covered all the things which we hadn't been able to talk about before, and we came to a mutual agreement that we would sit down and talk whenever either of us felt a need for it. But I don't want to imply that we won't have to continue working on it. Nothing is ever that easy, but at least we have developed a better understanding of how to keep the communication open."

"Sounds like the counseling experience was pretty successful."

"I think so, not only in opening up communication but also in allowing us to see things differently. She recognizes now she can't walk out and slam the door, and I know that I can't expect to keep the same controls over her as I've had in the past. She is an adult, and I must allow her to control her own life, even though she is living in my home."

"To me, that sounds like a lot of progress was made. Thank you for sharing this with me. I always thought your kids were perfect and you wouldn't understand if I told you about my problems with Tony."

"I'd like to hear about Tony. Why don't we go into the house and have a cup of coffee while you tell me about him?"

Rising from his chair, Ken said, "Great! I'd also like to hear what you think about my making an appointment at your church for Tony and me to see one of the peer counselors. Having a close father-son relationship would be good for both of us."

MOLLY: WORKING THROUGH GRIEF

"We had been married for thirty-five years when my husband died," Molly, the woman who was leading the group, said. In spite of the visible pain in her eyes, her face revealed the inner glow of a loving, caring person. She seemed to model a sense of tranquillity and confidence others in the group desired to emulate.

"Is that when you began this group for people like us who have suffered a real loss?" asked Jody, the young mother who had recently seen her only child die of leukemia.

"No, my husband died three years ago, and it has only been this year the group got started."

"I believe you told us that you have been working in the church's peer counseling program for eight years though," said Harry, the gray-haired man who lost his wife several months ago.

"That is correct. I was a peer counselor before, during, and after my husband's illness and death. In fact, having the support of the other counselors was so very important and helpful for me that I wanted people like you to have the same support I experienced. That is why I asked to begin this group."

"Then this group is a part of the total peer counseling program of the church," said Bob, a young man whose mother and father had both been killed in a tragic plane crash.

"That is correct. All of the peer counselors see their counselees individually, and some of us lead a group here at the church also."

"Are there similar groups who deal with other issues?" asked the recently widowed wife of the city's mayor.

"Yes, there are. Groups are meeting and dealing with many different life situations such as divorce, retirement, and single parenting. And if there is not an existing group and several people would like to attend one, then the director of counseling may approach a peer counselor about leading a new session."

"I think these meetings will be very important for me," said Jody, "but it is still very difficult for me to talk about my daughter. Since your loss is not as recent as most of ours, I wonder if you'd mind being first in telling us about your own experience?"

Realizing that it was important for trust to be built up in the group before others would feel like sharing, Molly answered, "Of course, I'll be glad to."

The circle of fifteen people grew very quiet as Molly began her story. "Stan had cancer, and it was a lengthy illness. His last years were a slowly winding down kind of a thing with a few emergencies thrown in. Thinking back on it, I guess it was just a period of time that we dealt with whatever we had to deal with. I can't remember a time that we were thinking about him dying. It's funny, one might think that would be uppermost in our minds, but it wasn't. It's as if you are in a different place at the time, and you think about what you have to do just on a day-to-day basis."

"In many respects I think that would be harder than losing someone suddenly like I did," Bob said.

"Maybe so. But you have to understand all the days during that two year period were not bad. Sometimes, Stan would go to the doctor or have to be in the hospital for a period of time. When he got back home he'd say, 'OK, now what are we going to do that's fun?' And we'd sit down and plan an outing, or even a short trip."

"It sounds like he was a fun-loving man. I know that makes good memories because my wife had the same up-beat attitude," said Harry.

"He had a lot of humor, and that was a tremendous help. In fact, the doctors didn't think that he would live the extra year he did, and I feel his positive attitude contributed to his time being lengthened."

"Do you feel that it was quality time?" Jody asked.

"Oh, yes. There were a lot of things that I had to help him do, but it was worth it."

"Do you mind talking about what kind of cancer he had?" Bob asked.

"Not at all. He had cancer of the throat. He was a smoker, and he didn't quit. That was something else I had to learn to deal with and accept. It was difficult for our son to understand why I couldn't get him to quit. I told him, 'This is your dad's choice, and it's his life.' I wouldn't let his smoking become a big issue with me because I don't believe that you can change another person. I spent a lot of evenings talking to all three of our sons during that time. They were grown and lived away from home, but we needed each other for support. I would start telling them how I was doing and how I felt, and then they would talk about feelings of their own."

"I didn't have anyone to talk to when our daughter was dying, because my husband was unable to deal with it at all. I did feel, though, that I was going through some of the grief even before she died," Jody said.

"I felt the same way," Molly said. "I felt like I went through some of my grief while I still had him. There was loss going on all the time, as I lost different parts of him. I remember telling a neighbor that I had lost him in pieces. He had a laryngectomy the year before he died, and that was one of the hardest things any of us in the family had to deal with because he lost his voice. I just did not realize how important hearing someone speak is. I could communicate with him, but I could not hear that voice I was so used to hearing. He wrote notes all the time, and I even found some after he died."

"Did he know how difficult not hearing his voice was for you?" Bob asked.

"Yes, I expressed my feelings to him about it. He good-naturedly made a joke out of it by turning my words around and saying that he'd like a little more of that from me. There really was a lot of humor in our lives. He may have been stubborn, ornery, and difficult at times, but for the most part, there was a real joyfulness about him. He was wonderful, and there were special things that he gave to all of us."

"Could you share some of those things?" Jody asked.

"Yes, of course. In my young married life, and later, he taught me a real independence. Over the years I developed many different interests from his. So when he died, I was able to slip back into the parts of my life that I already had. It made it easier for me. When he was living, we shared a love of travel, nature, reading—and we never ran out of things to talk about. I will always treasure those memories. But I am grateful we also had our independent interests. That was a gift he gave to me."

"You had been a peer counselor, and I presume you had been taught about death and loss. Were you prepared for his death?" Harry asked.

"Before he died, I had gone through a period of great sadness, tears, and frustration. But the strength from God through prayer, the support of a special group of peer counselors, and the love of family and friends gave me the courage and peace to deal with it all. When he died, there was a real sense that God was 'taking care of us.' It was a sense of relief and release."

"Did you go through the typical grieving stages?" Jody asked.

"I felt that I was a little farther along in the grief process because I had been able to deal with things all along. But one must go through all the stages of grief. If it is postponed, it will get you later. That is why your support of each other in this class will be so very important. I understand what you are going through, as you understand what each other is experiencing. In the weeks to come in these group meetings, we will talk out frustrations, vent anger, cry together, and support each other. We will remember the past, but we will also learn to look toward the future."

ELIZABETH: A TALENT FOUND

"I've spent a lot of years in church work looking for **my** talent," the attractive woman in her mid-forties confessed. Hesitating only briefly, she then continued, "The Bible tells us that

130

God gives each of us at least one talent, and I wanted desperately to find mine. I tried teaching Sunday school classes, working with youth groups, serving in the women's association—I tried a lot of different things before I found my talent. But now I've found it! And using it has brought me the most rewarding experiences of my life."

The group at midweek prayer services of the First Baptist Church were as interested and eager to hear their guest speaker as Fanny Clark had hoped they would be. After all, Elizabeth Stark was her niece, and for some time she had wanted her to share information about the peer counseling program which was being used so effectively at Faith Presbyterian Church. Now the opportunity had come, and Elizabeth had the audience captivated.

"I've always wanted to be a counselor. Even when I think back to my high school aptitude test, I remember it revealing that I should be a social worker. The way that I answered the questions indicated I'd be a good caretaker or helper. But for various reasons I decided to go another route, and for the past twenty years I've been an executive secretary in a bank. Now I get to be both a secretary and a counselor."

Elizabeth stopped and acknowledged a hand raised in the back of the room.

"How did you get started being a peer counselor?" asked seventy-year-old Mary Denton.

"I was attending a divorce workshop at church one weekend, and during the lunch break I met one of the peer counselors. He'd been serving in that capacity for several years, and he told me about the program and suggested that I apply. After lunch was over, I told him that I believed the Lord had brought me to the church that morning to hear about the peer counseling program, not to attend the divorce workshop. After making an initial application and attending an oral interview, I was accepted for the training."

"Does the training take very long?" A local city college student wanted to know.

"Various churches have different programs, each with their own requirements. I personally think we have one of the best programs, and I'll be glad to tell you about it. Every Sunday morning from March until October the initial training takes place. For two hours, instruction is given on the development of counseling skills. The group is led by a psychologist who volunteers his time. Books, as well as cassettes and video tapes, are used in the classes. After six months, each person is assigned to a veteran counselor who stays with the new peer counselor for the next three months while he is seeing counselees. It is only after this time that counselors are allowed to see counselees on their own."

"I remember when Mrs. Clark introduced you, she said that you attend training every Sunday morning from 6:30 until 8:30," Mrs. Winn recalled. "I find it hard to believe that anyone would get up that early on Sunday morning. Was she just joking?"

"No, she wasn't joking. For over three years, I've gotten up at five o'clock on Sundays. The training is continuous for all the peer counselors. We discuss various situations ranging from how to handle a counselee of the opposite sex when he or she might try to 'come on' to the counselor to how to deal with grief. These sessions are led by a volunteer psychologist who may stay for only one quarter or for the entire year. This meeting offers tremendous support for all the members in the group. It is too important to miss. So, we all get up early to attend."

"Could you give us an example of a person who might seek your services?" Judith Barnes asked.

"Yes, I work mainly with women and with couples who are having relationship problems. Some of my real success stories come from couples who have been on the verge of a divorce, but after months of meeting on a weekly basis and working very hard on their problems, they're now enjoying a happy marriage. I must tell you, though, peer counselors are not always able to bring about the results they hoped for. I remember one young couple who came to see me because of marital problems. After they had worked very hard for several months, it became apparent they could not find happiness together, so I helped them to work out an agreement of separation. We met four or five times to talk about issues from child support to selling their real estate to helping them look for separate quarters. I helped them to write out what they wanted their property settlement to be, so when they went to the attorney they wouldn't have such a high fee. Although we weren't successful at bringing the marriage back together, we were successful at helping two people go on with their own lives. The husband continued to meet with us for about six months after the divorce. He wanted help to avoid making the same mistake twice."

"Is there any time you feel you need to refer the case on to someone else?" Mrs. Black, a school teacher, wanted to know.

"Yes, we must report any child abuse cases to the proper authorities. Also, cases such as potential suicide, homicide, spouse abuse, or mental illness are referred to a licensed professional. The peer counselor is not prepared to deal with these kinds of problems. We are trained to recognize potentially dangerous situations, and we are quick to refer them to someone who is prepared to help."

"Suicide is so scary," interjected the high school senior, "I'd freak out if I had to talk to someone thinking of suicide."

"I know what you mean. I felt the same way before I had the peer counseling training. But we are taught to be aware of certain signs of potential suicide, and by 'picking up' on these we can get help for the person before the actual attempt is made."

"Yeah, that's neat!" the senior continued, "To know that you have helped save a life—that's awesome! But it's hard for me to relate to anyone who is so mixed up that suicide seems the only way out. That just seems so foreign to my thinking."

"The people who try to kill themselves are often people just like you and me who have just reached a real low spot in their lives. I know this is true because I once had a plan to kill myself."

The shock of the last statement was evident as the group grew very silent, with attention frozen on Elizabeth.

She continued, "I don't mind sharing something about myself with you. My life is really an open book. It's my life. I've lived it. I can't change it, but God knows that I've worked on trying to make it better." She paused momentarily before she said, "In my last divorce, I decided rather than be divorced again, I would take my own life. I had a plan in place. I was in therapy at the time because I knew myself well enough to know that I was in a deep depression and needed help. I had a list of seven people whom I was going to call before I did it. I wanted to tell them how much I loved them and say good-bye. I was seeing my therapist twice a week, and she would check with me each time to see how far down the list I had gotten. She knew the danger if I got to the bottom of the list. This sounds sick to me now, but I wanted to take my life on my husband's birthday. I thought my best gift to him was to give my life for him, to rid him of me. He had told me he was leaving me, and I didn't think that I could go through another divorce."

"But you seem so 'normal' now. No one would ever guess that you'd gone through so much!" a petite woman on the back row exclaimed.

"That is exactly the point. I am fine now, and I'm able to give back some of the things which have been given to me in the form of counseling and support. I'm sure that many of you have also had difficult lives, and you may be thinking that you would not qualify as a peer counselor. However, it may be easier to identify with another person if you have had a similar experience. That is why a peer counselor who is a widow may choose to talk to more new widows than any of her fellow peer counselors do. I know that I can identify with potential suicide victims, and with the support from my supervisor and my director of counseling, I've been effective in helping the ones I've seen. Life is not easy, and life experiences, along with proper training, may contribute to our being better peer counselors."

"Your honesty, dedication, and service are certainly to be commended," a woman in the audience remarked.

The high school senior nodded her head in agreement and then said, "You have been a peer counselor for nearly four years now, and I wonder if you ever think that you are giving too much when you donate nine or ten hours of work each week—too much of your time and talent without getting paid for it."

"No, that thought has never occurred to me because I've chosen to do it. Even if I've helped someone in only a small way, I've gained so much in return. I love what I'm doing. God has given me a talent to use for Him, and I'm very thankful that I've found that talent. I am constantly blessed by using it to glorify Him."

And because of Elizabeth Stark's talent and her willingness to share it with First Baptist, other people in that church will have an opportunity to find and use their talents in their own new peer counseling program. This program will grow from the seed planted on the night Fanny Clark invited her niece to speak at the midweek prayer service.

8

Peer Counseling
Ministry Models

History, theory, and abstracts have their place, but for many of us they will not have much meaning without a description of practical, working examples. Thus, this narration of the concepts undergirding peer counseling needs to be balanced with descriptions of tangible Christian peer counseling models. The ministry models presented in this chapter, then, illustrate the history, concepts, issues, and principles of the peer counseling movement. They provide true-to-life illustrations of the content of the previous chapters.

Thirteen models are included in this survey with the hope that its wide geographical sweep will allow readers some local reference and also facilitate networking between counseling programs. Continuing exchanges between programs also further advances peer counseling in the Christian community.

Peer counseling is flexible in structure and operation, hence it functions differently in various churches and parachurch organizations. There are subtle differences in the programs described on the following pages, but the common thread that makes each noteworthy is the love and care expressed toward hurting people and the desire to serve God.

Some of these programs refer to their participants by different titles—lay counselors, caregivers, encouragers, lay shepherds —but there is no question that their ministries are part of the peer counseling movement. Some programs follow what could be called a "traditional" style and structure of peer counseling, while others vary to some degree. This variety between programs is a testimony to the wide context in which peer counseling occurs and is a reminder to us that there are more than one or two ways to provide peer counseling services.

Peer counseling is in use in many denominations and faith groups. A conscious effort has likewise been made to include model ministries from as wide a range of denominations as possible so that helping individuals, churches, and parachurch organizations may find a source of ready identification with the peer counseling movement in their own denomination or interdenominational background. It is always encouraging to be aware of a sister church or a similar organization with a successful program in operation. Such awareness supports any individual or church with reservations about becoming the first (or only) to provide peer counseling in an area. The wide acceptance of peer counseling throughout the Christian community also promotes unity and kinship among believers who may not otherwise have such a common bond.

The descriptions that follow have been compiled from program brochures, sections of manuals, and correspondence. Addresses and telephone numbers are included for those who may want a more comprehensive understanding of these ministries. Some information was derived from journal articles and books. The bibliography of this book lists these information sources.

LAY COUNSELING MINISTRY OF THE
LA CANADA PRESBYTERIAN CHURCH
(Presbyterian Church, USA)
626 Foothill Boulevard
La Canada, California 91011
(818) 790-6708

The lay counseling ministry began in 1976 in this Los Angeles suburban church for the purpose of providing trained Christian helpers for the congregation and the community at large. It was established to serve people with special needs in times of concern, conflict, or crisis. The senior pastor, Dr. Gary Demarest, and Dr. David Bock, an elder and a clinical psychologist, founded the program, in concurrence with the church's governing board. An intensive training program was developed by Dr. Bock to train the laity for a paraprofessional level of counseling.

Administratively, the Lay Counseling Ministry is responsible to the Session of the church through the membership committee. A pastor of the church, Chuck Osborn, D.Min., serves as the director of counseling and is assisted by a supervising consultant who is a licensed mental health professional. This consultation is a commitment for a one-year period. There are also professionally trained clinicians who supervise the lay counselors, with a ratio of one clinician to two counselors. The lay counselors receive weekly supervision and training. All of the people in the program serve without compensation, with the exception of the director of counseling and a secretary who assists with intakes.

The Lay Counseling Ministry is publicized as a service to anyone who needs help with such concerns as grief, divorce, parenting, marital disharmony, broken friendships, job-related crises, conflicts with parents, and school problems. People are asked to contact the church for an appointment, at which time they are screened by the lay counselor intake administrator. Their need is assessed, and they are assigned to an available counselor. Referrals are made to community resources for the people requiring medical intervention or indepth psychological testing. Those who have a mental illness such as schizophrenia are also referred to an appropriate agency or hospital.

Appointments are kept at the church counseling offices

after the counselees complete the application process which includes a Lay Counseling Agreement Form. The form briefly explains the lay counseling ministry, discusses confidentiality and exceptions, and notifies the counselee that a reassessment may be made at the end of ten sessions. The form is signed by adults or the parent or guardian of a minor.

The lay counselors are members of the congregation, drawn from a wide variety of backgrounds and occupations, and have gifts, skills, and experience in supportive helping. The application process for becoming a lay counselor has three phases: (1) the completion of a questionnaire with two personal references, (2) a group interview, with the director, supervising consultant, and other lay counselors, and (3) an intensive training program of over one hundred hours. After the group interview, a determination is made as to who may take the training. Those who successfully complete the third phase are asked to become lay counselors and commit themselves to six to eight hours per week of ministry involvement for a minimum of one year. Counselors are placed with a veteran lay counselor for the first three months of weekly sessions before they are allowed to provide service on their own. Each lay counselor signs a contract agreeing to counsel between two and four hours a week, to obtain one hour of supervision for every four hours of counseling, to attend a two-hour ongoing training session each week, and to participate in at least one lay counselor weekend retreat per year. Currently there are more than twenty lay counselors in service.

Regarding records, the lay counselors are asked to keep confidential progress notes on a program form. These notes are reviewed in supervisory sessions. A termination/referral form is completed by the counselor when appropriate. Quarterly program reports are prepared by the director for the church's membership committee. A monthly financial statement is maintained by the church treasurer and presented to the governing board.

Counseling is provided without fee, but donation envelopes are available in the counseling offices for free will contributions. The 1987 program budget was over $4,000 and included expenditures for training materials, workshops, a retreat, and printing.

LAY SHEPHERDING PROGRAM OF
FIRST BAPTIST CHURCH
(American Baptist)
228 North Main Street
Fall River, Massachusetts 02720
(508) 672-5381

First Baptist Church in Fall River, Massachusetts, is a 650-member congregation located downtown, serving a 140,000 metropolitan area. Rev. Donald S. Mier provides pastoral leadership and advisement for this church's helping ministry.

When the church visitor retired in 1980, the leadership of the church decided to use a lay shepherding model. Ten people were trained using two books:

The Caring Church: A Guide for Lay Pastoral Care, by Howard W. Stone (New York: Harper & Row, 1983).

Lay Shepherding: A Guide for Visiting the Sick, the Aged, the Troubled, and the Bereaved, by Rudolph E. Grantham (Valley Forge, Pa.: Judson Press, 1980).

After a seven-week orientation, each lay shepherd took on his or her special assignments. Four are hospital visitors, taking flowers from Sunday's service with them to the members who are hospitalized. Five are assigned to five or six homebound members whom they visit on a regular basis. One has a preference to be assigned special cases, such as family problems, death, and bereavement. Meetings of the lay shepherds for support and continued training are held periodically throughout the year. New classes for additional shepherds are

140

scheduled as needed. The current ten lay shepherds include a variety of church members, including deacons.

NEIGHBORS WHO CARE—LAY COUNSELING
MINISTRY OF THE NEIGHBORHOOD CHURCH
(Assemblies of God)
625 140th N.E.
Bellevue, Washington 98005
(206) 747-3445

In 1975, Rev. Jack Rozell and psychiatrist Ray Vath began the Neighbors Who Care program when the senior pastor was in limited service (due to total exhaustion). Rev. Rozell developed the program from his initial position as part-time program director and later as senior pastor for many years. Since 1981, an associate pastor, Thomas A. Neumann, M.Ed., has been the director of counseling. From the first training class of 100 enrollees, the church has trained more than 1,550 Christian paraprofessional lay counselors from more than 140 churches and organizations.

The purpose of this ministry is to provide help by means of trained Christian lay counselors and professional counselors to persons who desire to grow and find meaning in daily living. It has been established to meet the growing requests for help which are too numerous to be handled by the pastoral staff. This ministry is an expression of love to meet the problems of troubled people within a spiritual perspective.

According to the church's program brochure, the philosophy is based on the belief that (1) man is a unique creation of God's design, (2) physical, psychological, and spiritual wholeness is possible through the application of biblical and psychological principles, and (3) people who have experienced and learned how to love can be a means of healing to others.

This ministry seeks to offer help that is Christian, professional, and confidential in the areas of spiritual, personal, marriage, family, premarital, divorce, abuse, and grief-bereavement difficulties. All appointments are scheduled by the office receptionist under the supervision of the director of counseling. Initial interviews ("intakes") are conducted by professional supervisory personnel.

The training is conducted by qualified professional people from the congregation and community. The initial training consists of forty-two hours over a period of fourteen weeks. One and a half hours are spent in teaching and one and a half hours in small-group experience. The groups are facilitated by two lay counselors each. The knowledge and skill development of the training are organized around a Christian counseling course, "Agape Therapy," copyrighted by Dr. Jack Rozell.

The knowledge acquired focuses on spiritual assumptions and implications of the counseling process as well as therapeutic models, including Transactional Analysis, Reality Therapy, Integrity Therapy, and Prayer Therapy. The training develops competence in displaying (a) accurate empathy, personal genuineness, and nonpossessive warmth, (b) active listening skills, (c) problem-solving skills, (d) testing (administration and interpretation abilities), and (e) abilities in diagnosing of cases and presenting case histories. Personal growth experiences are enhanced through role playing, discussion of case histories, individual and group counseling, and co-counseling with the supervisor.

Counselors are appointed by the leadership after careful screening by the director and assistant director and final approval by the senior pastor. The use of tests, interviews, and biographical analysis may be used in the selection. Each person selected for the ministry is asked to sign a statement of commitment agreeing to ongoing training, supervision, and availability of three to four hours per week. Also, ministry personnel sign a statement of ethics which is adapted from the American Association of Pastoral Counselors.

The counseling ministry is under the administrative direction of the senior pastor and the church board of deacons and elders with regard to program policy, finances, and facilities. The senior pastor appoints the director and assistant director. An advisory board, consisting of pastors, program staff, and consultants, assist the director in the operation of the program. Professional supervisory staff have responsibility for ongoing counseling by doing intakes, assigning lay counselors to counselees, and approving all referrals to other counseling resources. The supervisors meet with lay counselors and counselees every three to four weeks to give guidance.

Supervision of all counseling and lay counselors is within the guidelines of a counseling contract, with an emphasis on "short-term" and referral counseling. The program maintains confidentiality under all circumstances, except where legally obligated by law to report suicide, bodily harm to self, homicide, and child abuse.

Finances for the program are met by a church budget and donations of counselees. A sliding-scale donation schedule is used in the program, but services are provided for those who are unable to pay.

CHRISTIAN COUNSELING MINISTRY
OF THE ELMBROOK CHURCH
(Nondenominational)
777 South Barker Road
Waukesha, Wisconsin 53186
(414) 786-7051

Begun in the late 1970s, this program grew out of a need identified within a large women's Bible study taught by the pastor's wife, author Jill Briscoe. When women began approaching her for counseling, she referred them to professionals but soon became aware that many of the problems did not require intensive and expensive help. Thereafter, psychologist David Hubbard developed a lay counselor training program, which continues in existence today under the direction of Rev. Dick Robinson, associate pastor and pastoral coordinator of the counseling ministry. This program operated during its early years to serve women only, but during the early 1980s it expanded to serve men. The ministry now seeks to serve the three thousand adult members of the church and also community people living in the greater Milwaukee area.

According to the manual, the purpose of the counseling ministry is to maintain a lay spiritual counseling program, under the authority of Scripture, accountable to the council of elders, and consistent with evangelical theology. The principle functions of the counseling ministry are (1) to serve as a lay counseling referral resource for the pastoral staff and the ministry activities of the church, (2) to educate the church concerning issues of spiritual and emotional growth of consequence to the church and contemporary society, and (3) to nurture the spiritual, intellectual, and emotional growth of participants in the counseling ministry.

The leadership team of the ministry includes a pastoral coordinator, a counseling consultant, a counselor supervisor, a training director, an education coordinator, a growth groups coordinator, and a referrals coordinator. All of these positions are voluntary, with the exception of a salaried pastoral coordinator and the consultant on a retainer.

A church member becomes qualified to counsel upon completion of a training program and acceptance by the counselor supervisor. The person agrees to (1) a one-year, renewable commitment to the counseling ministry following training, (2) a personal devotional life, spiritual fellowship, and corporate worship experience, (3) participate in a counselor growth group for a minimum of nine months, (4) participate in in-service workshops, (5) be available to counsel with at least one client, and (6) participate in a supervision group while engaged in counseling.

A two-year counselor training program covers the areas of discipleship and spiritual growth, basic theology and biblical principles of counseling, integration of theology and psychology, counseling skills, and specific issues in counseling. The class members meet biweekly for two hours during the first year of training, and classes emphasize Christian truth

144

and discipleship principles. During the second year particular attention is given to personal growth and the development of Christian counseling skills. Role-playing exercises are used more extensively, and resource people conduct one-session seminars. Some class members are assigned counselees during this time.

After the two-year training program, the counselors are regularly involved in group activities. Support groups facilitated by lay counselors provide encouragement, insight, and practical assistance to counselors. Growth groups are led by volunteer professionals or experienced lay counselors to encourage personal and emotional development. Supervision groups for those with counseling case loads are facilitated by volunteer, professional counselors.

In 1987, the lay ministry served more than one hundred counselees. This ministry is a vital link in a counseling system which includes pastoral and professional counseling. The lay counselors are integrated into total church ministry by liaison to such target groups as single parents, the chemically dependent, working mothers, widows, and AIDS-related victims and families. Additional ministry networking is accomplished through a telephone counseling service.

ENRICHMENT BUILDERS LAY COUNSELING
PROGRAM FIRST BAPTIST CHURCH
(Southern Baptist)
Box 1158
Jackson, Mississippi 39205
(601) 949-1949

Enrichment Builders is a program designed and started in 1984 by the minister of counseling, Ron G. Mumbower, Ed.D. The stated purpose is to train lay people to become effective people helpers. This lay counseling service seeks to build up the children of God and equip the saints to provide the ministry of reconciliation to the hurting people they come in contact with every day. The theme verse for this program is:

Build Up, Build Up
Prepare the Road
Remove the Obstacles
From My People
(Isa. 57:14)

According to church leadership, the need for the program began with the vast numbers of people within the church who were barraging the minister of counseling. He could not possibly meet the demands of everyone, so he saw the need of training their laity to use their skills within their families, Sunday school classes, neighborhoods, and offices.

Enrichment Builders is a fifteen-hour course scheduled each winter quarter during the Sunday evening Church Training time, prior to evening worship. The group is composed of ten to fifteen members. Effort is given to choose people from all sections of the six-thousand-member church, including married couples, senior adults, single adults, college students, divorcees, and widows. The training program covers personality understanding (through the use of Taylor Johnson Temperament Analysis, Myers Briggs, or Adult Personality Inventory), basic counseling, influencing skills, encouraging actions, and grief and crisis (suicide and telephone) counseling.

Upon completion of the training course, the person is presented with a certificate and then encouraged to find his or her place in the church's helping ministry. The lay counselors provide the leadership for seven support groups, a telephone ministry on Sunday mornings, an engaged couple enrichment program, a newlywed Sunday school class, and parenting programs. At times these counselors are sent referrals by the minister of counseling.

After five years of program operation, there are more than fifty trained counselors in the church. Many of these have received advanced training, and some are serving in other churches.

PEER MINISTRY OF THE CHRIST
MEMORIAL LUTHERAN CHURCH
(Missouri Synod Lutheran)
9712 Tesson Ferry Road
Affton, Missouri 63123
(314) 631-0304

The peer ministry program for this congregation was begun in 1986. Marilyn Bader, director of programs and youth ministry, is the coordinator. It was instituted to help laity become better equipped to handle the difficulties with which friends, spouses, family members, and coworkers are confronted. Trainees are chosen in one of several methods: invitation from the trainer after the initial training, recommendation by those already trained, suggestion from the pastors, and by an open invitation issued to anyone in the congregation interested in receiving training. Class instruction is open to anyone willing to commit to learning a better means of helping others cope with pain and suffering.

The program at Christ Memorial has a two-tract approach: one training for youth and another for young adults and adults. The rationale for the two tracts is to equip the different age groups with skills and responses to deal with the issues typical of each age category. A third peer ministry for older adults (55+ years) is planned for this parish in 1989.

Both of the current tracts have parallel components. The initial training requires between twenty-five and thirty-five hours, depending on the size of the group, age, and maturity of the members. The adult and youth agendas are similar for the core curriculum. The subject areas are relationship development skills, conversational guidelines, attending skills and facilitative responses (questioning, listening, reflective responding, nonverbal communication, I-messages), decision making and problem resolution, dealing with sensitive issues, knowing and setting personal limits, problem ownership, and referral skills.

Subsequent training sessions of five to ten hours are scheduled to cover additional topics and skills not included in the initial training time. These sessions usually deal with more specific topics such as death and dying, grief and loss, substance abuse, confronting abusing friends, and sexuality.

The major differences between the two tracts occur in the role-playing and simulation experiences and values clarification discussions because of the differences in nature and depth of problems which occur at various ages. Other differences occur when working with grief and loss, parenting concerns, and substance abuse issues.

Various resources have been used to develop the curriculum for both age tracts. Dr. Barbara Varenhorst's *Curriculum Guide for Student Peer Counseling Training* (1980) is the primary instructional material. This resource is used as part of the peer ministry program sponsored by the Board for Youth Services for the Lutheran Church, Missouri Synod (1333 S. Kirkwood Road, St. Louis, Missouri 63122). Other class lessons are adapted from *Natural Helpers: A Peer Support Program* (1982) by Jane Akita and Carol Mooney, as well as *Caring and Sharing: Becoming a Peer Facilitator* (1978) and *Youth Helping Youth: A Handbook For Training* (1979) by Robert D. Myrick and Tom Erney.

Following training, counselors are encouraged to reach out in ministry to others in their natural networks, whether they be within their own family system, work place, school, or friendship circles. Several church-sponsored outreach ministries are available for those counselors willing to continue their service beyond the original commitment. These include:

1. CARE Team (*C*hemical *A*ddiction *R*eferral and *E*ducation)—a group of individuals committed to supporting and educating the congregation and community in substance abuse matters. Team members are available for crisis calls and referrals to local counselors,

treatment facilities, and programs specializing in addiction recovery.

2. VIP (Visitors Information Place)—a ministry operating from a centrally located booth at the church where visitors, guests, and prospective members can obtain information about the parish, its worship life, and opportunities to participate in the fellowship of the congregation.

3. Small group home Bible studies—additional training is available for counselors to understand group dynamics, Bible study, and discussion skills.

STEPHEN MINISTRY PROGRAM OF THE
UNION UNITED METHODIST CHURCH
(The United Methodist Church)
7582 Woodrow Street
P.O. Box 705
Irmo, South Carolina 29063
(803) 781-3013

Union United Methodist Church is a 2,500-member church in a suburban community of Columbia, South Carolina. In 1985, the church leaders began a lay care-giving program which was affiliated with the Stephen Ministries. This church is now one of 298 Methodist congregations nationwide enrolled in this organization. Jan Buck serves as the coordinator of the church's program, under the supervision of the associate pastor, L. Carroll Pope.

Developed in 1978 by Rev. Kenneth C. Haugk, the St. Louis, Missouri-based Stephen Ministries now has enrolled more than twenty-one hundred congregations in fifty-three denominations throughout forty-nine states, seven Canadian provinces, and four foreign countries. According to printed information, the Stephen Series is a system of training and organizing lay persons for caring ministry in and around their congregations. A local church becomes a "Stephen Ministry

149

Congregation" by payment of a one-time enrollment fee and by keeping the terms of a covenant. The fee includes tuition at a twelve-day leader's training course, continual update of new materials, and ongoing consultation as needed from the Stephen staff.

An associate pastor of the Union United Methodist Church, Nancy Donny, initially started the program with thirty members enrolled. In the second year, a new class of eighteen members began, while the first class of Stephen Ministers was commissioned to serve. These caregivers participated in a continuing education class and small-group supervision during the time of their service. A third class was begun in 1987 with twelve enrolled, and a fourth started with fourteen in 1988. Currently there are twenty-two Stephen Ministers in the program.

The present lay woman coordinator was employed by the church in 1988 to work on a part-time basis after a church staff decision was made to have the program operated by the laity. The program was strengthened by this reorganization.

Each Stephen Minister has completed fifty hours of training. Examples of some of the class subjects covered during the six-month period are feelings—yours-mine-and-ours, the art of listening, assertiveness, grief, confidentiality, crisis theory and intervention, ministering to older persons, what to do in the first helping contacts, and ministering to shut-ins. Part of the training sequence was a retreat which focused on such subjects as depression and suicide.

Commissioned caregivers were involved in continuing education classes for a six-month period with the curriculum covering problems in marriage, the effects of divorce on children, building self-esteem in others, personality development, transference, and child abuse. Outside resource people were used for some of these classes.

Primary instructional resources for the program include the *Stephen Series Leader's Manual* and the *Stephen Series Trainee Manual.* These materials are published by the national organization, and the local congregation leaders use these copyrighted resources in accordance to guidelines and permissions authorized by Stephen Ministries.

The Stephen Ministers agree to serve for a minimum of two years and provide care giving for an hour a week with one or two "helpees." Referrals come primarily from the pastoral staff and members of the congregation. The caregivers serve a variety of people's needs including the hospitalized, the bereaved, the elderly, those in job crises, the lonely, the inactive in the congregation, and new members.

THE SHEPHERDING MINISTRY OF THE
FIRST CONGREGATIONAL CHURCH
(United Church of Christ)
2 Main Street
Hopkinton, Massachusetts 01748
(508) 435-9581

The First Congregational Church is located in a community thirty-five miles from Boston. Dr. Richard A. Germaine, senior pastor, is committed to an active and equipped lay ministry in this evangelical church. He has served in his present position for seventeen years. Robert Cloutier is associate pastor and is administratively responsible for The Shepherding Ministry. In past years, there have been lay associate pastors trained to do visitation, counseling, and to lead small groups for fellowship, instruction, support, and prayer.

The Shepherding Ministry of the church includes geographical shepherding to the congregation in approximately twenty-three communities, a small group ministry called Covenant Groups that meet weekly with ten to twelve people in each group, an Elderly Shepherding Ministry, and the Agape Ministry for the mentally and physically disabled.

As a vital part of the Shepherding Ministry, a premarital counseling service has developed. In 1984, eight lay counselors were trained to meet with engaged couples before their wedding and to continue with this support for the first year after marriage. The counselors invite the couples into their own homes for discussion and to be participating observers of a Christian marriage and family life. Part of the counselor training involves the use of the Taylor-Johnson Temperament Analysis. A manual for premarital counseling has been developed for this successful program. It is presently being duplicated in a mission church, New Hope Chapel in Westborough, Massachusetts.

In October 1986, sixteen people enrolled in a new Prayer Team ministry. The purpose of the team members was to learn to minister to people in prayer through listening to them, helping them learn to pray, and interceding for them.

Pastor Germaine places a strong emphasis on spiritual gifts and seeks to lead his congregation in ministries that express these gifts. New members are encouraged to identify their gifts, and they are given a list of current ministries of the church. Such ministries in the recent past have included counseling, assistance to the elderly, hospital visitation, prison ministry, food and clothing for the needy, and work with the deaf. The Deaf Church of Hopkinton is a ministry of the First Congregational Church.

THE NORTH HEIGHTS LUTHERAN CHURCH COUNSELING CLINIC
(Evangelical Lutheran Church in America)
2701 North Rice Street
Roseville, Minnesota 55113
(612) 484-2049

The Counseling Clinic of the North Heights Lutheran Church was founded in 1977 by William Backus, Ph.D., clinical psychologist and associate pastor of the church. The clinic began serving clients in 1978. Dr. Backus has provided leadership to this ministry since its inception, and he continues to train and supervise lay counselors. Norman Fisk currently serves as the lay administrator of the counseling clinic.

Along with Dr. Backus and Rev. Fisk, the staff of the clinic consists of a secretarial and administrative assistant and a physician. The remainder of the staff includes the trained Christian lay counselors. All of the clinic staff serve without compensation. The more experienced counselors are assigned to supervise those recently trained.

Counselor selection includes interviews by the instructor, administrator, or a senior counselor before final approval at the end of the training program. Part of the selection process is the writing of a brief essay wherein the trainee summarizes his or her reasons for the call to service in the clinic.

The sixteen-week training program currently has ten two-hour sessions before actual counseling is scheduled. The counselor trainee receives instruction regarding conducting sessions, setting goals, and developing treatment plans. In the class sessions, there is a presentation of psychological disorders and the use of diagnostic tests. A textbook for the training is *Telling the Truth to Troubled People* (1985) by Dr. Backus. This book presents a counseling model called Misbelief Therapy, a Christian adaptation to cognitive-behavior therapy.

It is mandatory that all approved counselors continue in semimonthly training and supervisory meetings. The clinic staff has developed a Counselor Performance Evaluation form to validate knowledge, planning, skill development, and participation in the program. All counselors are subject to ongoing evaluation by videotape, recorded sessions, or supervisor observation.

Counselors see clients at the church offices only on Thursday evenings by prior appointment. New clients are given appointments for intake at the church office. Ongoing appointments are made by the counselor assigned to the client. Each lay counselor schedules two clients during the evening. As many as fifty clients may be seen by the counselors each week. A client attends an average of eight to ten sessions.

All clients who consent are administered the Minnesota Multiphasic Personality Inventory (MMPI). Used for diagnostic purposes, the counselor is trained to communicate the test results to the client.

The counselors are encouraged to use goal setting charts with the client, as well as a client self-evaluation chart. To facilitate the process of Misbelief Therapy, some counselees are assigned to read the book, *Telling Yourself the Truth* (1980) by William Backus and Marie Chapian.

In 1988, the budget for this Thursday Evening Clinic was approximately $4,000. The counseling service is free; however, the clients do pay for the MMPI and the self-help book. Donations are accepted from clients, and contributions are received from interested people. The clinic operates on a self-sustaining program budget.

THE LAY ACADEMY OF THE
EPISCOPAL DIOCESE OF CALIFORNIA
1055 Taylor Street
San Francisco, California 94108
(415) 673-2183

The Lay Academy provides training for volunteer laypersons from congregations in the Episcopal Diocese of California in facilitation and pastoral care skills. Persons are equipped to lead a group of peers in discussing their experiences around a particular issue with the goal of providing support to one another in the context of the good news of the Gospel. Nancy Axell serves as dean of the Lay Academy.

Pastoral Care, a six-session course, teaches listening skills, an understanding of Christian ministry, and care for caregivers. From this pastoral care course, two peer groups were formed in a local congregation.

Two people trained in pastoral care started a support group in their congregation called Children of Aging Parents. This group of six people met once a month for two years. The format they used included prayer for themselves and their parents, a sharing of how things were going, exercises or readings from the pastoral care course, distribution of various helping

154

resources, discussion, and closing prayer. On various occasions, the members called in a resource person to give insights into the elderly and to help with their perceptions of their aging parents. The group ended when all the parents had died.

A widows' grief support group provided peer ministry in the same congregation. The structure consisted of prayer, meditation, sharing experiences, exchanging resource materials, and discussion.

A diocesan-wide workshop entitled Breaking through the Blues, which sought to break self-destructive patterns caused by mild depression in women, was followed by a training for leaders of ongoing support groups. Instructor for this workshop and training was Marie Morgan, author of *Breaking Through*. This event was cosponsored by The Lay Academy and the United Church of Christ's Women Network. Many groups were formed and met for ten weeks, including one which continued at a local church for several years.

A peer-support group for the unemployed was developed and strengthened by a diocesan two-day employment symposium. This church peer group provided help in combating depression and in writing and critiquing résumés.

The Lay Academy has trained lay people to lead congregational support groups of five to twelve persons around the issue of making choices in the workplace through a decision-making process concerning ethical dilemmas at their job site.

NEW DIRECTIONS COUNSELING CENTER
(Parachurch and Paraprofessional
Organization)
996 Oak Grove Road
Concord, California 94518
(415) 798-7500

Founded in 1974 by psychologists Robert C. Richard, Ph.D., and David Flakoll, Ph.D., the New Directions Counseling Center was incorporated to serve as a crisis and short-term counseling service for low-income people. It now also serves clients from abusive backgrounds and is more long-term in the number of counseling contacts. Currently, one of the fastest growing services is work with troubled children and adolescents. Judy Thompson has served as the executive director for the past three years. She is a paraprofessional staff member who has provided counseling services at the center throughout its years of operation. Dr. Richard continues to serve as a consultant and trainer.

This nonprofit, public benefit organization exists as an extension of area churches' counseling ministry in the San Francisco Bay region. At the onset of the program, an invitation was extended to churches in Contra Costa County to recommend persons who would be interested in the lay counselor training program. A screening process was established that included the use of personality inventories and measures obtained through evaluating current helping abilities. As part of the application process, prospective counselors submitted brief written statements as to why they wanted to become lay counselors. Thirty-six persons from many different Christian denominations were accepted in the first training program.

The stated goal of the center is to improve the level of emotional, social, and spiritual functioning of individuals experiencing moderate emotional distress, a personal crisis, or breakdown in relationships and to be an extension of the churches' counseling ministry. Basic services offered include individual, couple, family, and group counseling. Information and referral is provided as needed. According to an intake policy, the center does not accept people with severe suicidal tendencies, psychotic reactions, or chronic chemical addictions unless the addicts are in a recovery program.

New Directions Counseling Center utilizes a substantial number of Christian volunteers to provide its services and operate the organization. More than a thousand hours are donated each month.

A fifteen-member volunteer board represents a broad base of the Christian community, and all members chair or sit on a working committee. At least two counselors from the center serve on the board at all times.

Thirty-six trained Christian paraprofessional counselors, eleven college interns, and two newly licensed Marriage, Family, Child counselors (MFCC's) provide individual, marriage, family, child, and group counseling on a volunteer basis. In addition, two receptionists and the librarian donate their hours to the center.

Private-practice professionals supervise the eleven interns on a one-to-one basis, eight consultants act in an advisory capacity, and an intern gives psychological testing to clients when needed. All volunteer their time.

The salaried executive director is immediately responsible to the board of directors. Professional counselors provide services under the direction of the clinical director, Del Olson, D.Min. The lay counselors are directly responsible to the clinical director and their immediate supervisor.

Prospective paraprofessional counselors are required to take a twenty-four-week training course given by two psychologists and meeting for three hours a week. This course is paid for by the trainee (approximately $400). Personal psychological tests are given to each member before and after the course, and those who are interested in counseling at the center are then carefully screened before being accepted as counselors. Basic training includes "How to Develop a Helping Relationship," "Self-Awareness," "Elements of the Counseling Interview," and "Techniques of Counseling."

Four professionals with marriage, family, and child counseling licenses supervise the forty-seven paraprofessional counselors. Each supervision group meets two hours a week and is comprised of no more than eight counselors.

The Training and Education Committee of the Board meets and plans bimonthly advanced training seminars for the counselors and interested community members on all areas of counseling, such as battered women, child abuse, alcoholism, marriage counseling, dealing with adolescents, and drug abuse.

Since this service is designed for use by persons unable to afford available professional counseling, the fee is $20 per session. In those cases where this fee is still a hardship for the person, it will be lowered, $1 being the lowest fee.

The funding for the ministry comes from churches, an annual fund-raising event, the United Way, foundations, corporations, and individual donations. New Directions is eligible to receive endowments, memorials, and wills.

A recognition of the success of this paraprofessional counseling ministry is indicated by the fact the center twice received the coveted J. C. Penny Golden Rule Award for outstanding volunteer service to the community, and the most recent award was won in 1988. Many community leaders visit the New Directions Center to learn about the program. The ministry model has been replicated by two new Christian, nonprofit organizations: Community Counseling Center in Napa, California, and Calvary Bible Church in Grass Valley, California.

LOVE LINES, INC.
(Parachurch and Paraprofessional
Organization)
2701 S.E. Fourth Street
Minneapolis, Minnesota 55414
(612) 379-1199

Love Lines was founded in March 1972, by Christian businessman Dan Morstad and other interested lay people. A significant development occurred in 1973 when Dan and Diane Morstad, along with a small group of Christian counselors, worked together to answer telephone calls resulting from a local rock radio program. This media event mixed rock music with an evangelistic message and invited people who wanted counseling to telephone. From that small beginning, the flood of calls from hurting people opened the door to a twenty-four-hour crisis telephone ministry in 1977. Presently, the Morstads are codirectors of the organization.

Love Lines is a nonprofit, interdenominational, and evangelical ministry. The central mission of Love Lines is the twenty-four-hour-a-day, seven-days-a-week teleministry serving people of the Twin Cities area. A related ministry is the Blessing Center which was begun in 1980. It now provides both physical and spiritual assistance for those needing clothing, employment, furniture, or food. Financial counseling to help people manage their money is available on a one-on-one basis. Another ministry is the In-Person counseling service for those who need or want continued assistance with problems over a longer period of time. In 1985, Love Lines launched a weekly family television program on a local cable station. Hosted by the Morstads, this ministry is designed to provide Christian answers for daily living. The organization's telephone number is given to viewers for counseling and follow-up help.

The Reverend Dan Morstad is president of Love Lines' five-member board of directors. A direct mail and computer specialist is employed full time. This is the only paid position in the organization other than that of the codirectors. The office staff consists of a full-time secretary and two part-time bookkeeping and accounting personnel. Other volunteers serve in five departments: (1) administration, (2) personnel, (3) evangelism, (4) prayer, and (5) development.

The director of training and the director of counseling work in the personnel department. The training director recruits counselors and prepares them for service. The director of counseling is responsible for counselor scheduling, support, and evaluation.

Requirements for becoming a counselor include the following: the completion of an application along with a pastor's recommendation, an interview with the director of training, and the completion of two phases of the training program. The first phase consists of classroom instruction and discussion for a two-month period. Phase two is a four-month period of classroom training and an internship. At this point the counselor may be certified for telephone ministry. Counselors must be eighteen years and older.

Continued training is available in phases three and four. Telephone counselors are required to participate in phase three, ongoing education. This includes two hours each week of group instruction and support. Phase four is designed for those people who wish to qualify for the In-Person counseling ministry. These advanced counselors will have completed one year of supervised telephone counseling, three months of additional training, and an evaluation process.

Love Lines provides in-depth training from its manual emphasizing counseling skills based on the Scripture, prayer, and an acknowledged concern for others. A variety of mental health literature from a Christian perspective is used in the program, and outside speakers are scheduled on a regular basis. The counselors are taught to use a prayer and counseling report form, which records identifying information and program service statistics.

In 1987, telephone calls to Love Lines numbered more than 63,000. For the first six months of 1988, the total telephone calls were 30,313. Selected categories of concern were salvation inquiries, 369; suicide, 319; drug and alcohol, 626; family, 4,052; mental/emotional, 4,706; financial, 1,474; and sexual problems, 496. These statistics are reported from time to time in the Love Lines' quarterly newsletter.

No fee is required for service, but donations are accepted. Funds are received from individual and church contributions, special fund-raising events, donations from people served, and philanthropy from community organizations. In 1988, the operating budget was $132,000.

A teen line is to be developed in the near future using trained, Christian teenage counselors.

MATCH-TWO (M-2) PRISONER OUTREACH
(Paraprofessional Organization)
Statewide Headquarters
500 Main Street, P.O. Box 447
San Quentin, California 94964
(415) 457-8701

In late 1971, a group of concerned citizens presented a plan to the California Council of Criminal Justice and the Department of Corrections proposing that they would enlist volunteers from the community to visit incarcerated men, women, and youths who had few or no visitors. The volunteer would be a friend to someone who had no friends.

This group, then called Job Therapy of California, a non-profit organization, began with pilot programs in the state prisons at San Quentin, Folsom, Tracy, and Vacaville. The program, now known as Match-Two (M-2) Prisoner Outreach, has active programs in 35 correctional institutions throughout California and has made 32,809 matches during the period from 1971 to 1988. According to their annual report, the M-2 program has grown to be the largest and most effective one-on-one prisoner visitation program in the country. Heading up the M-2 program is Samuel M. Huddleston, president and chief executive officer.

Match-Two's goals are to recruit and equip volunteers from the community to provide caring relationships for prisoners in the California system who apply for such a match. Inmate and volunteer applications are reviewed by Match-Two program directors at each institution and appropriate "matches" are then made. Volunteers agree to visit their inmate at least once a month and to write letters in the intervening time.

Match-Two volunteers must be at least twenty-one years of age and have an ability to offer genuine care and faithful friendship. The program matches men with men and women with women. The staff provides orientation and training for

161

volunteers and ongoing monitoring and support throughout the matching relationship. The effectiveness of the matching process is dependent upon the dynamics of a caring human relationship and positive role modeling.

Recent studies show that 80 percent of today's crimes are committed by persons who have previously been incarcerated. A study conducted by the California Department of Corrections in 1987 documented that Match-Two parolees who had had twelve or more visits from Match-Two volunteers had an 81 percent better parole success than those inmates who had not participated in the program. This means that fewer Match-Two parolees return to prison than those who have not participated in the program.

The services of Match-Two volunteers in 1987–88 totaled 286 volunteer hours per day, a net worth of $1,001,939 to the state and community at large for the year. The annual cost to the system of keeping an adult inmate is approximately $19,000. For an annual cost of $262 (the cost of making one successful match), Match-Two can provide the necessary services to drastically reduce recidivism.

Annual revenues for the Match-Two program are nearly $2 million, with funds coming from the state of California contracts, foundation grants, corporate philanthropy, church contributions, individual donations, and organizational fund-raising events.

Administratively, the Match-Two statewide program has a ten-member board of directors and a staff leadership team consisting of a president, program director, director of marketing and planning, finance director, executive secretary, and regional directors. Throughout the state of California, there are more than twenty-eight area directors and volunteer staff who coordinate services and provide public relations to the community. The program has an active liaison to the California Department of Corrections, California Youth Authority, and the Federal Bureau of Prisons.

The positive friendship so essential to Match-Two programs is fundamentally a peer-to-peer relationship. Effective sponsors need the same care and communication skills that are the core of a good peer counseling program. While training in the program may differ throughout the state, depending on staff orientation, peer counseling concepts such as active listening, nonjudgmental attitude, empathy, and support are being used in equipping the sponsors.

Many Christians from various denominational churches are involved in the Match-Two program. Church leaders have demonstrated a strong support for the program. Many Match-Two staff regard churches as a ready resource for recruitment of sponsors and visit churches for this purpose. The program has a seventeen-minute multimedia presentation which is used in community and church awareness programs. Therefore, many volunteers respond to the invitation of Matt. 25:36, "I was in prison and you came to me." Thus Christians are well motivated to serve as peer counselors in a program like M-2.

Part 4

Working Aids

9

Sample Forms and Program Ideas

Having resource material that is proven and practical is usually instructive and helpful. Thereby, the practitioner benefits from the insights and ideas of others. Forms and aids have been selected from various peer counseling ministries to illustrate how a concept, principle, policy, or procedure appears in a specific working ministry. Those desiring more tools or guides may contact the ministry leaders associated with the models presented in this book.

The forms shared in this book appear in the following order (the source behind each genericized form is given in parenthesis):

1. Sample of a personal interview data form
   (Neighbors Who Care Lay Ministry, Bellevue, Wash. [hereafter listed as Neighbors Who Care])

2. Sample program announcement
   (Lay Counseling Ministry, La Canada Presbyterian Church, La Canada, Calif. [hereafter listed as Lay Counseling Ministry])

167

3. Program idea (philosophy of ministry section)
   (Christian Counseling Ministry, Elmbrook Church, Waukesha, Wis. [hereafter listed as Christian Counseling Ministry])

4. Sample trainee application
   (People Helper Peer Counseling Program, Vista Grande Church, San Diego, Calif. [hereafter listed as People Helper Program])

5. Sample donation policy declaration
   (Neighbors Who Care)

6. Program idea, an interest/availability statement
   (People Helper Program)

7. Sample release of liability form
   (Counseling Resource Center, First Presbyterian Church, Boulder, Colo.)

8. Sample intake information form
   (Lay Counseling Ministry)

9. Sample job description (director)
   (Neighbors Who Care)

10. Program idea, release permission form
    (Lay Counseling Ministry)

11. Program idea, a prayer and counseling report form
    (Love Lines, Inc., Minneapolis, Minn.)

12. Sample counselee referral form
    (Christian Counseling Ministry)

13. Sample job description (assistant director)
    (Neighbors Who Care)

14. Sample evaluation form
    (Lay Counseling Ministry)

15. Sample counselor evaluation form
    (North Heights Lutheran Church Counseling Clinic, Roseville, Minn.)

Sample Forms and Program Ideas

1. SAMPLE OF A PERSONAL INTERVIEW DATA FORM

Personal Interview Data   Date _____

Name _____ Phone _____

Address/City/State/Zip _____

_____

Occupation _____ Business Phone _____

Age/Birthdate _____

Marital Status: Single _____ Engaged _____ Married _____
A steady involvement _____ Widowed _____ Divorced _____
Separated _____ How long? _____

Is your spouse willing to come in for counseling?
                    Yes _____ No _____ Uncertain _____

Education (Last year completed): _____

Other Training (List type and years): _____

_____

Referred here by _____

Health Information

List significant illnesses (past and present), injuries, or handicaps:

_____

Are you presently taking prescription medication? Yes ___ No ___

If yes, what medication are you taking and for what? _____

Are you currently using alcohol and/or drugs? Yes _____ No _____

If yes, which and how frequently? _____

Have you experienced any changes in sleeping or eating patterns recently? If yes, please describe:

_____

If you have recently suffered the loss of someone who was close to you, indicate the relationship to you and when this occured:

_____

Have you recently suffered loss from serious social, business, or other reversals? Yes _____ No _____ Explain: _____

_____

_____

Are you currently seeing a counselor or psychotherapist?
Yes _____ No _____ If yes, list the counselor or therapist's name and phone number.

Name _____ Phone _____

Briefly describe your involvement with your church: _____

_____

Marriage Information

Name of Spouse _____

Address _____

Phone _____ Occupation _____

Business Phone _____ Your Spouse's Age _____

Education (in years) _____ Religion _____

Date of Marriage _____

Your ages when married: Husband _____ Wife _____

Have you ever been separated? Yes _____ No _____

Filed for divorce? Yes _____ No _____

How long did you know your spouse before marriage? _____

Length of steady dating with spouse _____

Length of engagement _____

Give brief information about any previous marriage: _____
_____

Information about Children

*PM	Name	Age	Sex	Living Yes No	At Home/ On Their Own	Marital Status

*Check this column if by previous marriage

Briefly answer the following questions

1. What is the nature of your concern?

2. What have you done about it?

3. What can we do? (What are your expectations in coming here?)

4. As you see yourself, what kind of person are you? Describe yourself.

5. What, if anything, do you fear?

6. What other information would you like us to know?

7. Have your recently thought of taking your own life or the life of another? Describe:

2. SAMPLE PROGRAM ANNOUNCEMENT

Could counseling by a lay counselor help you?

Do you feel Boredom?
Discouragement?
Frustration?
Despondency?
Depression?
Loneliness?

Counseling helps with feelings triggered by:
Grief
Divorce
Parenting
Marital disharmony
Broken friendships
Being new in town
Assertiveness
Handling anger
Drug-Alcohol abuse
Job-related crises
Conflict with parents
School problems

Counseling is for everyone. We all could use counseling from time to time. Strength comes in sharing.

Counseling is confidential. You need have no reluctance in discussing your intimate feelings with a trained lay counselor. (They have spent more than one hundred hours in training.)

Counseling is available during daytime or evening hours.

Counseling is nonjudgmental. Your counselor will not evaluate nor preach to you. He will accept you as you are.

To set up an interview—Simply call [counseling service number] and say, "I'm _____. Please ask one of the lay counselors to call me at [your number]." That is the church office phone. Call during business hours on weekdays or between 9:00 and 11:30 on Sundays.

3. PROGRAM IDEA (PHILOSOPHY OF MINISTRY)

A. Biblical principles.

1. Every Christian is a new creation in Christ Jesus. (2 Cor. 5:17)
2. This new life is given through our reconciliation by God, with God. (2 Cor. 5:18)
3. Reconciliation with God is the model and the hope for our reconciliation with one another. (Eph. 2:14–18)
4. The goal of Christian personal growth is to become complete in Christ. (Col. 1:28)
5. God is committed to completing this process of growth in us. (Rom. 8:28–30)
6. Personal transformation begins through a process of renewing the mind. (Rom. 12:2)
7. Personal transformation continues through a lifestyle of obedience to God. (John 14:15ff.; 2 Cor. 1:12)
8. God's grace is sufficient for living with our weakness when problems seem irresolvable. (2 Cor. 12:9)
9. All psychological theories must be brought under the authority of Christ and Scripture. (2 Cor. 10:5)

B. Practical and theological principles.

1. All truth is God's truth.
Academic and clinical psychology, when coherent and consistent with the revealed truth of Scripture, can offer helpful insights into human needs, as well as techniques for the meeting of human needs. Where personal growth is inhibited or emotional problems persist because of past psychological damage, we will refer to competent professional psychologists.

2. Self-esteem is dependent upon rightly understanding mankind's relationship to God.
As human beings, we are dependent upon God for our existence

As human beings, we are dependent upon God for our existence and a sense of acceptance and personal well-being. We have been created in God's image and therefore have a basic need for a sense of identity and worth. We find our self-esteem in forgiveness for sin and acceptance by God in Christ Jesus. We will resist all self-love and self-help psychologies that do not account for sin and atonement and personal transformation through Christ.

3. Human beings are a unity of body and soul.

Mankind has been created by God as "living beings," into whom God has breathed "the breath of life." As such, we are both material and immaterial; both are necessary for us to be human. There are various interrelated aspects of our personhood including, but not limited to, the spiritual, intellectual, emotional, and social life.

4. As people differ in background and personality, so they will respond differently to different counseling techniques.

Our basic counseling technique is to listen empathetically and help people find within themselves and in their relationship to God, the directions necessary to resolve or cope with their personal problems. Apart from that, we recognize that some people will respond better to some counselors than others and profit more from some counseling approaches than others.

5. In order to find fulfillment, people need to live in rightly ordered relationships with God and with other people.

Personal Christian growth is the cornerstone to living rightly in our various relationships. We will strive to uphold the sanctity of life, fidelity to the marriage covenant, reconciliation in relationships, and integrity in personal lifestyles in our counseling.

4. SAMPLE TRAINEE APPLICATION

Name: _____ Sex: _____

_____ _____
(Address)   (Telephone)

Age: 16–19   20–25   25–40   40–60   60+

Place of Birth: _____ How long lived in this area: _____

I am: Single   Married   Divorced   Remarried   Widowed

I am a: Parent   Steparent   Foster Parent   Adoptive-Parent

How long have you been a Christian? _____

Church member: Yes _____ No _____

How long have you been attending this church? _____

Highest educational level: _____ Diplomas: _____

Degrees/certificates: _____

Occupation: _____ Length of employment: _____

Employer: _____
(Name of Company, Agency)

_____
(Address)

Hobbies and leisure-time interests: _____

_____

Organizations, clubs, and associations: _____

_____

Counseling Experience: Formal   Informal   Describe: _____

_____

_____

_____

Type of person(s) most capable to counsel?

Children   Adolescents   Young Adults   Adults   Singles

Marital Couples   Families   Elderly   Parent-Child

Comments: _____

_____

_____

Time availability for counseling: _____
(hours a week)

_____
(days and time each week)

Time concerns: _____

Training Program

I am interested in the basic People Helper class because _____

_____

I am interested in the advanced People Helper seminars because

_____

Specific contributions you can make to the training program ____

_____

_____

_____

Additional information or comments: _____

_____

_____

_____

_____

_____

_____

_____
(Signature)

- -

Date application received _____

By whom _____

Additional information: _____

_____

Disposition: _____

5. SAMPLE DONATION POLICY DECLARATION

For your information and understanding please read and initial this form.

This counseling ministry has had the privilege of sharing the love and truth of Jesus Christ with several thousand people who have come to us for help in the fourteen years of our service. It is the vision of the church leadership and congregation for this ministry to continue and expand as the Lord leads.

We deeply value you, our pastoral and lay leadership, and the calling God has put into our hearts. Your financial support is an expression of how you value this ministry as well. With your financial investment in your own help, you put a stronger value on the helping process, and it is healthy for your own growth as well. No one will be turned away for lack of ability to make donations. However, we ask that you put value on this ministry in the form of financial responsibility/support.

Look over the Donation Schedule and circle the amount that corresponds to your family net (take home) income/size. This will not commit you but gives us a place from which to start. In the initial "intake" interview, the pastoral supervisor will work with you to identify the donation responsibility that we can together agree upon and commit to for the succeeding sessions. This will be reviewed at each supervisory session, which is normally once per month.

Donation envelopes are available for you on the reception area counter in the office. We request that you turn in your donations to the receptionist prior to each session. Make checks payable to "The Church." Your cancelled check is your receipt for charitable contribution income tax purposes. Cash receipts will be provided to you upon request from the receptionist. Thank you.

———————
Initial here

Donation Schedule
Requested per Session

Net (Take home) Income *per month*	Number in family (Parents, children, dependents)					
	1	2	3	4	5	6 or more
Below $ 600	5	5	5	5	5	5
$ 601–$ 800	10	9	7	5	5	5
801– 1000	15	14	12	10	8	8
1001– 1200	20	19	17	15	10	10
1201– 1500	25	24	22	20	15	15
1501– 1700	30	29	25	22	20	20
1701– 1900	35	34	32	30	25	25
1901– 2100	40	39	37	35	30	30
2101– 2300	45	44	42	40	35	35
2301– 2500	50	49	47	45	40	40
2501– 2800	55	54	52	48	45	45
Above 2801	60	59	57	55	50	50

More Facts and Figures

This church congregation has invested more than $xx,xxx in this ministry during its years of existence. Support from those who have been helped has been approximately $xx,xxx. Church leadership has long struggled with this lack of support. They have now given us a directive to facilitate increased financial responsibility/support from those helped, recommending a minimum $25 Intake donation.

Donations are expected to balance out completely the following budget items:

administration
supplies/materials
professional consultation
operations/facilities
workshops/seminars

179

insurance
honorarium to professionals for lay counselor training
professional affiliation
books/videos/cassette tapes/testing materials

This is where your responsibility lies. Tithes and offerings from the church congregation pay for the pastoral supervisor salaries but do not cover these items. These costs ($xx,xxx–$xx,xxx/yr.) need to be covered by your generous donations. Thank you in advance for cooperating with us in this concern!

Sample Forms and Program Ideas

6. INTEREST/AVAILABILITY STATEMENT

Date: _____

Name: _____

Address: _____

Telephone: _____ Preferred times to contact you: _____
                (home)

_____

Please state your future *availability* for service.

_____
_____
_____

Please describe your special *interests* as to type of people or situations you prefer as a people helper.

_____
_____
_____

Would you be willing or able to assist in the training of others in future introductory classes?

_____ Yes _____ No   Comments: _____

_____
_____

Will you be participating in the advanced people helper seminars?

_____ Yes _____ No   Comments: _____

_____
_____

Additional remarks: _____

_____
_____

181

7. SAMPLE RELEASE OF LIABILITY FORM

The counseling service offered at _____ is a response to personal or family needs based on the Christian understanding of giving ourselves to our neighbors. The lay counselors have received training in the skills of listening, clarifying, and goal setting from Christian professionals trained in marriage, family, and child counseling; they are not professionals in psychological counseling or psychiatric therapy.

I understand and agree that the contacts I shall have with the lay counselor(s) are not professional, but that the counselor is receiving professional supervision with my consent. I also understand that our meetings may extend up to ten sessions. After that time there shall be reassessment and a new decision concerning the best course of action.

Permission for Counselor to Receive Supervision through Audio and Videotapes, Observation, and Records

I understand that the communication between me and my counselor is confidential, and that no information regarding me will be shared, either verbally or in written form, with any other person except as allowed by agreement below.

To aid the supervision of my counselor, I agree that audio or video recordings of our sessions may be made and viewed by my counselor's supervisor, clinical consultant, or other counselor, and that they also may observe sessions either by attending or through a one-way window and may read all written records pertaining to our counseling. At no time will sessions be recorded or observed without my knowledge.

_____   _____
Signature   Date

_____   _____
Signature   Date

_____   _____
(If under eighteen, parent or guardian)   Date

182

8. SAMPLE INTAKE INFORMATION FORM

1st Appt. Date   Supervisor:
  / /   Counselor Availability:

Counselee(s):

Name(s)	*Age*	*Sex*	*Marital Status*	*Occupation*
_____	__	__	_____	_____
_____	__	__	_____	_____
_____	__	__	_____	_____

Address: _____ City _____ Zip _____

Phone: (home) (____) _____ (work) (____) _____

Referred from: _____ Check back: Yes ____ No ____

Church Preference/Affiliation: _____

Donation Arrangement: _____

Medical Information:

Physician's name: _____ Phone: (____) _____

Medication (kind and dosage): _____

Significant illnesses/operations: _____

Alcoholic intake: Daily _____ Weekly _____

Recreational Drug Use: _____

Prior Counseling:

When/For/Counselor: _____

_____

Presenting Problem of Counselee(s): _____

Details: _____

_____

_____

_____

9. SAMPLE JOB DESCRIPTION FOR DIRECTOR OF
PEER COUNSELING PROGRAM

Director of _____ will be responsible for the total organization of the total counseling program. The director will have weekly consultations with the senior pastor regarding present programs, new programs, and functional concerns.

Responsibilities

1. Makes decisions regarding ongoing matters and has general oversight regarding referrals to outside agencies. Confers with and procures the services of consultants and is the liaison person between them and this ministry.

2. Supervises the responsibilities of the assistant director. Assigns specific responsibilities and work schedules. Meets weekly to discuss plans, programs, and responsibilities. Shares information regarding new services available and changes in the procedure.

3. Counseling
   Tasks: Intake counseling
   Crisis counseling
   Supervises lay counselors, supervisors, and support group leaders
   Keeps abreast of latest resources for referrals
   Makes referrals to other agencies

4. Coordinates the ministry of our lay counselors
   Tasks: Leads supervisory meetings
   Provides for in-service training
   Establishes a calendar of these ministries
   Works with the resource persons involved

5. Serves as chairman of the counseling advisory council
   Tasks: Leads supervisory meetings
   Provides for in-service training
   Establishes a calendar of these ministries
   Works with the resource persons involved

6. Oversees the financial expenditures of the counseling ministry program by establishing its budget and approving its expenditures
   Tasks: Meets with business manager on a regular basis
   Discusses major expenditures with the pastor

7. Supervises counseling interns who are involved in this ministry
   Tasks: Interview
   Works cooperatively with the college course guidelines
   Assigns tasks
   Checks monthly report
   Submits a quarterly report to the college

8. Works in the ongoing supervision of supervisors
   Tasks: Individual consultations
   Share suggestions and changes during advisory council meetings and lay counseling meetings

9. Establishes support groups and supervises the support group leaders and programs
   Tasks: Meets individually as needed with the leaders until the program is established
   Meets monthly with the leaders
   Receives monthly reports from each leader
   Keeps a file on each support group
   Provides up-dated articles, materials, and information to assist the individual programs

10. Plans workshops and seminars to broaden the scope of the church body and assure outreach to the community
    Tasks: Plans programs, contacts speakers
    Arranges for brochures, mailings, and deliveries
    Requests rooms, equipment, and assistants
    Initiates correspondence, advertising, and announcing
    Hosts programs
    Evaluates (How can we improve?)

11. Chairman of the Grants Committee
    Tasks: Calls meetings when advisable
    Supervises volunteer grants writer
    Provides materials and information of foundations
    Keeps file of foundations appropriate to specific needs
    Assistant administrator types letters as needed

12. Arranges for publications in news media and television
    Tasks: Promotes public relations for special occasions
    Meets with individuals when necessary in planning audio-video materials within the church and/or community as it pertains to counseling (Cooperatively with the pastor)
    Relies on assistance of volunteer media specialists

13. Confidential Files
    Tasks: Obsolete files shredded. Name and tag filed only
    Ongoing files are checked randomly to assure date is related to process rather than subjective opinion
    Consistently reminds supervisors to observe lay counselor data and insure appropriate comments

14. Supervises counseling secretary's duties
    Tasks: Utilizes the services of the secretary and volunteer secretary
    See job description

15. Plans monthly lunch meeting with consulting physicians
    Tasks: Assures that reservations are confirmed and doctors are attending
    Plans agenda
    Implements suggestions

16. Professional Growth
    Tasks: Constant reading to up-date knowledge, skills, approaches, and community resources
    Attends workshops and conferences
    Contacts other counseling programs, churches, and

186

        agencies to keep abreast of progress in relation to
        community needs

        Reads latest journals, indexes, and files—shares infor-
        mation

        Consults with experts of various fields as necessary

        Relies on all types of news media to update awareness
        of needs and/or resources

        Keeps an open mind for progress within the guidelines
        of this ministry

17. Evaluation
    Tasks: Ongoing evaluation of all programs, meetings, and
           daily routine

10. SAMPLE RELEASE PERMISSION FORM

_____ has my permission to release to
(Agency or Counselor)

_____ the confidential information on
(Receiving Agency or Counselor)

_____.
(Counselee's Name[s])

The released information will inform _____
(receiving agency or counselor)
about the educational, medical, psychological, and/or counseling

services which _____ received
(counselee)

from _____
(agency or counselor)

and will be used by _____ in order to
(receiving agency or counselor)

assist in the counseling for _____.
(counselee)

This authorization for release of confidential information is valid

from the date the form is signed until _____.

_____   _____
Date   Counselee/Parent/Guardian/Conservator

_____   _____
Date   Second Parent/Guardian/Conservator, if
                            legally responsible for Counselee

11. SAMPLE PRAYER AND COUNSELING REPORT FORM

Start Time _____ Counselor's Name _____

End Time _____ Date _____/_____/_____

Length of Call _____ Shift _____ to _____ A.M./P.M.

Please circle A.M. or P.M.

☐ Mr & Mrs	NAME (first, middle, last)
☐ Mr	ADDRESS
☐ Mrs	
☐ Miss	CITY ... STATE ZIP CODE
☐ Ms	
☐ child	PHONE ... MAIN
☐ other	CODE

Constant caller _____ Occasional caller _____

Matt. 6:33   But seek first the kingdom of God and all of his righteousness, and then all these things taken together will be given you besides.

1. What is your relationship with Jesus?   ☐ Knows Jesus
                                            ☐ Never Met

   ☐ Prayed for salvation?

   ☐ Prayed for Baptism of the Holy Spirit?

   ☐ Wanted follow-up (Church, Paraclete, Healing team)

2. We have a helpful free brochure on your situation. I'd like to send it to you.
             newsletter ☐   literature ☐☐☐☐

3. We are in need of prayer counselors, receptionist, computer input typists, and office help. Is there an area in which you could help?

☐ Counseling   ☐ Office   ☐ Other _____

☐ 15 minutes a day prayer clock _____ to _____ A.M./P.M.

_____

_____

_____

_____

189

12. SAMPLE COUNSELLEE REFERRAL FORM

_____

Date

_____

Referring Pastor

1.

Name _____

Address _____ City _____ Zip _____

Phone: [H] _____ [W] _____

2.

Age	☐ Single ☐ Married ☐ Divorced ☐ Children
___	

No. Years Mo/Yr Name Age
_____ _____ _____ ___
Spouse
_____ ___
_____ ___
_____ ___

3.

Reason(s) for seeking counseling:

_____
_____
_____
_____
_____

Previous counseling: ☐ Yes ☐ No _____ _____
                                    When   Where/Who

Availability: M T W Th F S Day Eve Time _____

Call: xxx-xxxx

190

13. SAMPLE JOB DESCRIPTION FOR ASSISTANT DIRECTOR OF
PEER COUNSELING PROGRAM

Assistant Director of _____ is directly responsible to the director of counseling; is assigned specific responsibilities and hours to assure appropriate supervisory coverage and consults weekly regarding programs, plans, and needs.

Responsibilities

1. Arranges for fourteen-week lay counselor training
   Tasks: Scheduling
            Planning
            Advertising
            Correspondence
            Provides materials and set-up of equipment
            Supervises facilitators

2. Counseling
   Tasks: Intake and Crisis Counseling
            Supervises assigned lay counselors and file reports
            Refers to outside agencies
            Utilizes confidential release forms as necessary

3. Supervises counseling interns
   Tasks: Interview
            Works cooperatively with the college course guidelines
            Assigns tasks
            Checks weekly or monthly report
            Submits a quarterly report to the college

4. Coordinates the counseling offerings for the elective classes in the Adult Development and Training program
   Tasks: Determines area of need for counseling training
                classes cooperatively with the director
            Contacts teachers
            Arranges for room and equipment

5. Purchases books, tapes, and educational materials
   Tasks: Submits purchase orders for approval
            Keeps records of purchases

6. Attends monthly consultation lunch meetings with physicians
   Tasks: Assures mutual confidentiality forms are on file for clients discussed
   Works cooperatively with the resource physician

7. Professional Growth
   Tasks: Constant reading to up-date knowledge, skills, and approaches
   Attends college classes
   Attends workshops
   Journals, news media, conferences
   Contacts with other churches and agencies

8. Correspondence pertinent to job description
   Tasks: Utilizes counseling secretary
   Dictates letters
   Information for monthly mailer and bulletins
   Handles registration for lay counseling training
   Keeps records

9. Plans workshops and seminars to broaden the scope of the church body and to assure an outreach to the community
   Tasks: Providing input and ideas
   Taking part in all phases of the programs

10. Self-Evaluation
    Tasks: Keep records
    Record activities
    Check: Are the lay counselors under my supervision becoming more mature in skills, approaches, and their ability to see objectively? Are clients responding? Do facilitators exhibit a greater awareness of the groups climate and individual needs? Are there changes occurring? Am I pre-planning to facilitate a smooth flow within the structure and organization of each task?

11. Weekly consultation

14. SAMPLE EVALUATION FORM

Supervisor Name: Counselor Name(s):

_____   _____

_____

1. Please describe one or two strengths of our ministry.

2. Please describe one or two ways in which you believe our ministry might be improved.

3. Please fill in the following counselor evaluation form. (If you had two counselors, designate one [X] and the other [0].)

	Deficient	Below Peer Level	Peer Level	Above Peer Level	Excellent	Insufficient Information
Makes good use of supervision	1	2	3	4	5	X
Evaluates his/her own performance	1	2	3	4	5	X
Accepts feedback from peers and supervisor (non-defensiveness)	1	2	3	4	5	X
Raises questions	1	2	3	4	5	X
Reports problems	1	2	3	4	5	X
Incorporates suggestions	1	2	3	4	5	X
Keeps progress notes up-to-date	1	2	3	4	5	X

4. Please write any additional comments you have about your supervisee or the Lay Counseling Ministry. If more space is needed, use the back of this sheet.

15. SAMPLE EVALUATION FORM OF COUNSELOR

Client _____ Counselor _____

Observer _____ Date _____

Listening Skills: (Rate on 5 point scale; 1 being poor, 5 being excellent)

1. Posture
2. Eye contact
3. Nonverbal attending behavior

(Record number of times counselor uses these response/techniques, make any comments in space provided)

4. Restatement of content
5. Paraphrasing/summarizing content
6. Reflection of feelings
7. Open questions
8. Closed questions
9. Primary questions
10. Secondary questions
11. Neutral questions
12. Leading questions
13. Clarifying
14. Perception checking
15. Identifying themes

Other comments / encouragement / critique / suggestions / favorite recipes

Bibliography

Adams, Jay E. *Competent to Counsel.* Grand Rapids, Mich.: Baker Book House, 1970.

————. *Ready to Restore: A Layman's Guide to Christian Counseling.* Grand Rapids, Mich.: Baker Book House, 1981.

Backus, William. *Telling the Truth to Troubled People: A Manual for Christian Counselors.* Minneapolis, Minn.: Bethany House, 1985.

————. "A Counseling Center Staffed by Trained Christian Lay Persons." *Journal of Psychology and Christianity* 6, no. 2 (Summer 1987): 39–44.

Baldwin, Carl Less. *Friendship Counseling: Biblical Foundations for Helping Others.* Grand Rapids, Mich.: Zondervan Publishing House, 1988. See Leader's Guide, pp. 259–309.

Becker, Walter W. "A Delivery System within the Church: A Professional Consultant and the Laity." In *Is There a Shrink in the Lord's House? How Psychologists Can Help the Church,* edited by H. Newton Malony, 83–88. Pasadena, Calif.: Integration Press, 1986.

————. "The Paraprofessional Counselor in the Church: Legal and Ethical Considerations." *Journal of Psychology and Christianity* 6, no. 2 (Summer 1987): 78–82.

Benner, David G., ed. *Baker Encyclopedia of Psychology.* Grand Rapids, Mich.: Baker Book House, 1985.

Bernbaum, John A., and Simon M. Steer. *Why Work? Careers and Employment in Biblical Perspective.* Grand Rapids, Mich.: Baker Book House, 1986.

Billy Graham Evangelistic Association, Spiritual Counseling Department. *Christian Worker's Handbook.* Minneapolis, Minn.: World Wide Publications, 1981.

Bobgan, Martin, and Deidre Bobgan. *How to Counsel from Scripture.* Chicago: Moody Press, 1985.

Bryant, Marcus D. *The Art of Christian Caring.* St. Louis: Bethany Press, 1979.

195

Bustanoby, Andre. *Being a Single Parent*. Grand Rapids, Mich.: Zondervan Publishing House, 1985.

Caplan, Gerald, and Marie Killiles. *Support Systems and Mutual Help: Multidisciplines Explorations*. New York: Genne and Stratten, 1976.

Carkhuff, Robert R. *Helping and Human Relations: A Primer for Lay and Professional Helpers*. 2 vols. Amherst, Mass.: Human Resource Development Press, 1983.

————. *The Art of Helping VI*. Amherst, Mass.: Human Resource Development Press, 1987.

———— et al. *The Art of Helping* (Video Series). Amherst, Mass.: Human Resource Development Press, 1986.

————, and W. A. Anthony. *The Skills of Helping*. Amherst, Mass.: Human Resource Development Press, 1979.

Carr, John C., John E. Hinkle, and David M. Moss III, eds. *The Organization and Administration of Pastoral Counseling Centers*. Nashville, Tenn.: Abingdon Press, 1981.

Clebsch, William A., and Charles R. Jaekle. *Pastoral Care in Historical Perspective*. New York: Jason Aronson, 1964.

Clinebell, Howard, Jr. *Basic Types of Pastoral Care and Counseling*. Rev. and enl. Nashville, Tenn.: Abingdon Press, 1984.

————. *Mental Health through Christian Community: The Local Church's Ministry of Growth and Healing*. Nashville, Tenn.: Abingdon Press, 1965.

Collins, A. H., and D. Pancoast. *Natural Helping Networks*. New York: National Association of Social Workers, 1976.

Collins, Gary R. *Can You Trust Psychology? Exposing the Facts and the Fictions*. Downers Grove, Ill.: InterVarsity Press, 1988.

————. *Christian Counseling: A Comprehensive Guide*. Rev. ed. Dallas: Word Publishing, 1988.

————. *Helping People Grow: Practical Approaches to Christian Counseling*. Santa Ana, Calif.: Vision House, 1980.

————. *How to Be a People Helper*. Santa Ana, Calif.: Vision House, 1976.

————. *Innovative Approaches to Counseling*. Resources for Christian Counseling, vol. 1. Waco, Tex.: Word Books, 1986. Especially chapter 4, "Lay Counseling," 71–87.

————. "Lay Counseling within the Local Church." *Leadership* 1, no. 1 (Fall 1980): 78–86.

————. *People Helper Growthbook*. Santa Ana, Calif.: Vision House, 1976.

————. *People Helper Pak*. Ventura, Calif.: Regal Books, 1976.

Crabb, Lawrence J., Jr. *Basic Principles of Biblical Counseling*. Grand Rapids, Mich.: Zondervan Publishing House, 1975.

————. *Counseling by Encouragement* (Video Series). Columbia, S.C., 1981.

Bibliography

———. *Effective Biblical Counseling: A Model for Helping Caring Christians Become Capable Counselors.* Grand Rapids, Mich.: Zondervan Publishing House, 1977.

———, and Dan B. Allender. *Encouragement: The Key to Caring.* Grand Rapids, Mich.: Zondervan Publishing House, 1984.

D'Andrea, Vincent, and Peter Salovey. *Peer Counseling Skills and Perspectives.* Palo Alto, Calif.: Science and Behavior Books, 1983.

Dayton, Howard L., Jr. *Your Money: Frustration or Freedom? The Biblical Guide to Earning, Saving, Spending, Investing, Giving.* Wheaton, Ill.: Tyndale House, 1986.

Detwiler-Zapp, Diane, and William C. Dixon. *Lay Caregiving.* Philadelphia: Fortress Press, 1982.

Dobson, James. *Love Must Be Tough: New Hope for Families in Crisis.* Waco, Tex.: Word Books, 1983.

Doering, Jeanne. *Your Power of Encouragement.* Chicago: Moody Press, 1982.

Drakeford, John W. *People to People Therapy.* New York: Harper & Row, 1978.

Egan, Gerald. *The Skilled Helper.* 3d ed. Monterey, Calif.: Brooks/Cole, 1986.

———. *You and Me: The Skills of Communicating and Reacting to Others.* Monterey, Calif.: Brooks/Cole, 1977.

Ehrenberg, Ott, and Miriam Ehrenberg. *The Psychotherapy Maze: A Consumer's Guide to Getting in and out of Therapy.* Rev. ed. Northvale, N.J.: Jason Aronson, 1986.

Friel, John, and Linda Friel. *Adult Children: The Secret of Dysfunctional Families.* Deerfield Beach, Fla.: Health Communications, 1988.

Friesen, Gary. *Decision-Making and the Will of God.* Portland, Oreg.: Multnomah Press, 1980.

Gartner, Alan. *Paraprofessionals and Their Performances.* New York: Praeger, 1971.

Gary, H. D., and J. Tindall. *Peer Counseling: In-depth Look at Training Peer Helpers.* Muncie, Ind.: Accelerated Development, 1985.

Grunlan, Stephen, and Daniel Lambrides. *Healing Relationships: A Christian's Manual for Lay Counseling.* Camp Hill, Pa.: Christian Publications, 1984.

Hart, Archibald D. *Feeling Free.* Old Tappan, N.J.: Fleming H. Revell Co., 1979.

Haugk, Kenneth C. *Christian Caregiving: A Way of Life.* Minneapolis, Minn.: Augsburg Publishing House, 1984.

———, and William J. McKay. *Christian Caregiving: A Way of Life* (Leader's Guide). Minneapolis, Minn.: Augsburg Publishing House, 1986.

Hightower, James E., Jr., ed. *Caring for Folks from Birth to Death*. Nashville, Tenn.: Broadman Press, 1985.

Hughes, Selwyn. *Helping People through Their Problems*. Minneapolis, Minn.: Bethany House Publishers, 1981.

Ivey, A. E. *Microcounseling: Innovations in Interview Training*. Springfield, Ill.: Charles G. Thomas, 1971.

Kennedy, Eugene. *Crisis Counseling: The Essential Guide for Nonprofessional Counselors*. New York: Continuum Publishing Co., 1986.

Kübler-Ross, Elizabeth. *On Death and Dying*. New York: Macmillan Publishing Co., 1969.

Larson, Dale, ed. *Teaching Psychological Skills: Models for Giving Psychology Away*. Monterey, Calif.: Brooks/Cole, 1984n

Lindquist, Stanley E. *Action Helping Skills: Manual for Peer Counseling*. Fresno, Calif.: Link Care Press, 1976.

———. *Reach Out: Become an Encourager*. Wheaton, Ill.: Creation House, 1983.

Littauer, Florence. *Blow Away the Black Clouds*. Rev. and exp. ed. Eugene, Oreg.: Harvest House Publishers, 1986.

———. *Your Personality Tree*. Waco, Tex.: Word Books, 1986.

Littauer, Fred and Florence Littauer. *Freeing Your Mind from Memories That Bind*. San Bernardino, Calif.: Here's Life Publishers, 1988.

Martin, Grant L. *Counseling for Family Violence and Abuse*. Resoures for Christian Counseling, vol. 6. Waco, Tex.: Word Books, 1987.

Miller, Paul M. *Peer Counseling in the Church*. Scottsdale, Pa.: Herald Press, 1978.

Moore, Joseph. *A Teen's Guide to Ministry*. Liguori, Mo.: Liguori Publications, 1988.

Morris, Paul. *Love Therapy*. Wheaton, Ill.: Tyndale House, 1974.

Myrick, Robert D., and Don L. Sorenson. *Peer Helping: A Practical Guide*. Minneapolis, Minn.: Educational Media Corporation, 1988.

Oden, Thomas C. *Crisis Ministries*. New York: Crossroad, 1986.

Olson, G. Keith. *Counseling Teenagers: The Complete Christian Guide to Understanding and Helping Adolescents*. Loveland, Colo.: Group Books, 1984.

Olson, Richard P., and Carole Della Pia-Terry. *Help for Remarried Couples and Families*. Valley Forge, Pa.: Judson Press, 1984.

Osborne, Cecil G. *The Art of Understanding Your Mate*. Grand Rapids, Mich.: Zondervan Publishing House, 1967.

Penner, Clifford, and Joyce Penner. *A Gift for All Ages: A Family Handbook on Sexuality*. Waco, Tex.: Word Books, 1985.

Platt, Larry A., and Roger G. Branch. *Resources for Ministry in Death and Dying*. Nashville, Tenn.: Broadman Press, 1988.

Bibliography

Prater, Jeffrey S. "Training Christian Lay Counselors in Techniques of Prevention and Outreach." *Journal of Psychology and Christianity* 6, no. 2 (Summer 1987): 30–34.

Richard, Robert C. "The Professional Counselor and Local Paraprofessional Mental Health Organizations." *Journal of Psychology and Christianity* 6, no. 2 (Summer 1987): 35–38.

Rozell, Jack V. "Lay Counseling in the Local Church." In *The Holy Spirit and Counseling,* edited by Marvin G. Gilbert and Raymond T. Brock, 103–19. Peabody, Mass.: Hendrickson Publishers, 1985.

Satir, Virginia. *Peoplemaking.* Palo Alto, Calif.: Science and Behavior Books, 1972.

Schaefer, Charles E., and Howard L. Millman. *How to Help Children with Common Problems.* New York: New American Library, 1983.

Schmitt, Abraham. *The Art of Listening with Love.* Nashville, Tenn.: Abingdon Press, 1982.

———, and Dorothy Schmitt. *When a Congregation Cares.* 2d ed. Scottsdale, Pa.: Herald Press, 1986.

Sheehy, Gail. *Passages: Predictable Crises of Adult Life.* New York: Bantam, 1977.

Smith, Harold Ivan. *Tear Catchers: Developing the Gift of Compassion.* Nashville, Tenn.: Abingdon Press, 1984.

Sobey, Francine S. *The Nonprofessional Revolution in Mental Health.* New York: Columbia University Press, 1970.

Somerville, Robert B. *Help for Hotliners: A Manual for Christian Telephone Crisis Counselors.* Phillipsburg, N.J.: Presbyterian and Reformed Publishing Co., 1978.

Southard, Samuel. *Training Church Members for Pastoral Care.* Valley Forge, Pa.: Judson Press, 1982.

Steil, Lyman K. "Listen My Students . . . And You Shall Learn." *Instructional Newsletter toward Better Teaching* (University of Minnesota) 11, no. 12 (Fall 1978): 1.

Stone, Howard W. *The Caring Church: A Guide for Lay Pastoral Care.* New York: Harper & Row, 1983.

Streiker, Lowell D. *Family, Friends, and Strangers: Every Christian's Guide to Counseling.* Nashville, Tenn.: Abingdon Press, 1988.

Strom, Kay Marshall. *Helping Women in Crisis: A Handbook for People Helpers.* Grand Rapids, Mich.: Zondervan Publishing House, 1986.

Sturkie, Joan. *Listening with Love: True Stories from Peer Counseling.* San Jose, Calif.: Resource Publications, 1987.

Sunderland, Ronald D. "Lay Pastoral Care." *Journal of Pastoral Care* 42, no. 2 (Summer 1988): 159–71.

Swihart, Judson J., and Gerald C. Richardson. *Counseling in Times of Crisis.* Resoures for Christian Counseling, vol. 7. Waco, Tex.: Word Books, 1987.

Tan, Siang-Yang. "Lay Christian Counseling: Present Status and Future Directions." Paper presented at the International Congress on Christian Counseling, Atlanta, Ga., November 1988.

————. *Lay Counseling: Equipping Christians for a Helping Ministry.* Grand Rapids, Mich.: Zondervan Publishing House, forthcoming.

————. "Lay Counseling: The Local Church." In *Is There a Shrink in the Lord's House?* edited by H. Newton Malony, 89–102. Pasadena, Calif.: Integration Press, 1986.

————. "Training Paraprofessional Christian Counselors." *Journal of Pastoral Care* 42, no. 4 (December 1986): 296–304.

Van Cleave, Stephen, Walter Byrd, and Kathy Revell. *Counseling for Substance Abuse and Addiction.* Resources for Christian Counseling, no. 12. Waco, Tex.: Word Books, 1987.

Van Ornum, William, and John B. Murdock. *Crisis Counseling with Children and Adolescents: A Guide for Nonprofessional Counselors.* New York: Continuum Publishing Co., 1983.

Van Wagner, Charles A., II. "Supervision in Lay Pastoral Care." *Journal of Pastoral Care* 31, no. 3 (September 1977): 158–63.

Varenhorst, Barbara B., with Lee Sparks. *Training Teenagers for Peer Ministry.* Loveland, Colo.: Group Books, 1988.

Wagner, C. Peter. "Wagner-Modified Houts Questionnaire for Discovering Your Spiritual Gifts." Pasadena, Calif.: Fuller Evangelistic Association, 1985.

Walters, Richard P. *Counseling for Problems of Self-Control.* Resources for Christian Counseling, no. 11. Waco, Tex.: Word Books, 1987.

Ward, Waylon O. *The Bible in Counseling.* Chicago: Moody Press, 1977.

Welter, Paul R. *Family Problems and Predicaments: How to Respond.* Wheaton, Ill.: Tyndale House, 1977.

————. *How to Help a Friend.* Wheaton, Ill.: Tyndale House, 1978.

————. "Training Retirement Center and Nursing Home Staff and Residents in Helping and Counseling Skills." *Journal of Psychology and Christianity* 6, no. 2 (Summer 1987): 45–56.

White, John. *A Christian Physician Looks at Depression and Suicide.* Downers Grove, Ill.: InterVarsity Press, 1982.

Wright, H. Norman. *Crisis Counseling: Helping People in Crisis and Stress.* San Bernardino, Calif.: Here's Life Publishers, 1985.

————. *Training Christians to Counsel.* Eugene, Oreg.: Harvest House Publishers, 1977.

Bibliography

Worthington, Everett L., Jr. "Issues in Supervision of Lay Christian Counseling." *Journal of Psychology and Christianity* 6, no. 2 (Summer 1987): 70–77.

———. *When Someone Asks for Help: A Practical Guide for Counseling.* Downers Grove, Ill.: InterVarsity Press, 1982.

Wynn, J. C. *The Family Therapist: What Pastors and Counselors Are Learning from Family Therapists.* Old Tappan, N.J.: Fleming H. Revell Co., 1987.